THE

Administrative

Process

THE

Administrative Process

BY

ROBERT H. ROY

The Johns Hopkins University

BALTIMORE
THE JOHNS HOPKINS PRESS

FOR

Mollie
and
Florrie

Foreword

THE appearance of a successful book on mathematics, or physics, or engineering is always *prima facie* evidence that the author is expert in the field about which he writes. This is the connotation of a book about administration too: to write the book at all, the author must himself be a skilled administrator. Of course, this need not be true and this book and this author pretend no such claim. Certainly there is no such thing as a perfect administrator, be he author or no.

Some of the case histories are of real situations and real people and it is possible that some may recognize themselves and the roles they have played. I do not think that I have been uncomplimentary or severely critical in any case—certainly not intentionally. On the contrary, to all who have contributed to my administrative insight, whether by accident or design, I am most grateful.

All of the chapters have been exposed to my graduate classes over the past half-dozen years and the manuscript has benefited more than a little from the discerning criticism of students. Some of the topics have been presented to groups of industrial executives, others to research groups, and still others to union-management meetings. I am not altogether sure who has taught whom on these occasions and must express gratitude for many ideas and shades of meaning derived from these sources.

More direct acknowledgement is due to Mr. Gordon Dalsemer, Vice-President, The Lord Baltimore Press, and Mr. J. Theodore Wolfe, President, the Baltimore Gas and

Electric Company. Chance discussions with each of these executives led to their reading certain portions of the manuscript and this in turn led to their review of each chapter as it was prepared. My good fortune in having their discerning assistance is warmly and gratefully acknowledged.

Closer to home, so to speak, has been the invaluable aid given by my colleagues and friends on the Johns Hopkins faculty, Drs. Sidney Davidson, Acheson J. Duncan, Charles D. Flagle, and Eliezer Naddor. It is more than pleasant to record my obligation to them and also to Mrs. Leonora Hunner, to Mrs. Thelma Hurley and to Mrs. Joyce Franke, who labored valiantly and successfully to produce a decent typescript from manuscript that was often an illegible mess. The finished manuscript was read by Mr. P. Stewart Macaulay, Provost of the University. It is pleasant to say thanks for his excellent comments and also to bow to a fine administrator.

An old and most valued friend, Mr. Robert S. Gill, Chairman of the Board of the Williams and Wilkins Company, read and corrected the entire manuscript and saved me from countless syntactical and rhetorical flaws. This labor has been shared by my wife, who also gave the patience and forbearance necessary and expected from all wives of would-be authors. Adequate thanks for obligations so close to the heart are hard to express.

Lastly, it is somewhat akin to coming home to have one's book printed by old friends at the Waverly Press and I am grateful for this too.

Baltimore
The Johns Hopkins University
October 1957

Contents

Illustrations

I

On the Administrative Process

S EVERAL years ago, in a small faculty group organized to appraise University departments, I remarked that industrial engineering has been primarily a clinical activity, inasmuch as its findings are based upon observation of existing situations, rather than upon controlled experiment. Somewhat to my surprise, for I was then new to academic life, several members of the committee expressed very critical opinions of clinical activities in general and of industrial engineering in particular.

Since then, I suppose by a natural process of self-justification, I have taken some consolation from the observation that numerous other, quite respectable fields of scholarship are clinical in various ways. The historian, the economist, and the political scientist all must base their findings and their theories upon observation of the body politic. Psychologists, sociologists, and to some extent psychiatrists have become experimentalists but much of their knowledge rests upon clinical observation and practice, and much continuing activity in these fields is of the same kind.

I cannot account for this contempt for a clinical field except by surmising that it comes from a current reverence for everything that is scientific or experimental or, perhaps, from intellectual snobbishness. It is also possible that it may derive from the mistaken belief that advancement of knowledge comes invariably through a sequence of experimental method, science, and then application for the benefit of society.

That this sequence has been followed in the development of such things as electricity and electrical engineering is not denied but in many other cases the reverse has been true: we have had art, practice, and advancement through experience and clinical analysis long before the emergence of an experimental method or a science. This has been the case, for example, with structures, built and carried to a state of truly remarkable development long before the appearance of experimental testing methods and deflection formulas. In the same way the steam engine was invented and improved by practitioners before Sadi Carnot, Willard Gibbs and others created a science of thermodynamics. Medicine remained simply the art of healing for centuries before the advent of controlled experiment and scientific method.

In this same connection one further point can be made. We do have a science of structures, a science of thermodynamics, and a science of medicine, but much of practice in these fields is still an art. The structural designer computes stresses and strains with precision—and then adds a safety factor. The creator of a heat engine cannot hope to achieve a successful design without those essential "hunch factors" that he has learned by clinical experience. No physician can practice medicine "scientifically," to the exclusion of the things that he has learned by that self-same practice. If one can argue that science gives birth to application, so also can one argue that just as often it is art, practice, and technology which give birth to science.

My purpose in belaboring these matters is to draw a parallel between them and administration. If one accepts the definition that administration is the leading or direction of an organization or a segment of an organization, then we surely have had administration as long as there have been organizations, and that is a very long time indeed. And, just as surely, we do not yet have a science of administration, such misnomers as "Scientific Management" to the contrary notwithstanding. Skillful administration is an art, refined and matured in the clinic of experience. Furthermore, if an experimental method and a science of administration are to emerge, perhaps through researches in the behavioral sciences, or through operations research, sound progress still will be dependent, as it is in medicine, upon clinical support.

These essays are born of experience and clinical observation of administration in action. That experience, moreover, has been relatively narrow: as an engineering staff executive in a small plant and as part of the administrative organization of a university. The scope of such experience, even though buttressed by the literature of administration, hardly qualifies me to argue, as I do argue, that the attributes of administration are essentially similar in all walks of organized activity: industrial, academic, social, military, mercantile, governmental, or religious. I shall not be able to prove this, of course, but do hope to be able to establish many points of identity.

2

Many—far too many—analyses of the administrative process take final expression in a series of "oughts." A production executive *ought* to forecast the activity of his machines, a superviser *ought* to communicate with his subordinates, there *ought* to be good will at the bargaining table, and so on, ad infinitum. A perceptive colleague has called these somewhat pious instructions "votes for virtue" and that is about all they are. Such platitudes are ubiquitous enough but repetition alone is not likely to provide better administrative practice. Opposition to sin does not make the world altogether virtuous.

Anyone writing about administration is bound to slip into voting for virtue from time to time, through inadvertence if nothing else. Certainly if one is to do more than analyze and diagnose, if one is to prescribe any therapy at all, some measure of "oughts" is inevitable. In any case, these pages do attempt some administrative therapy; it is hoped that emphasis is upon how and why such therapy should be exercised and not upon "virtue" alone. If platitudes do appear, they will have escaped the author, who asks pardon for them.

These essays, which begin in the clinic with a case history, make no claim to be comprehensive of the whole field of administration. They do aim to reveal some attributes of administration which appear to be neglected in practice and to have escaped analysis in the literature. Some of the topics have been borrowed for the purpose of amplification and exemplification; others represent my own ideas or, perhaps, are the sub-conscious expression of thoughts gleaned elsewhere. To all of these sources, known and unknown, I am very grateful.

II

On the Administrative Process

IN INDUSTRY, years ago, when serving as a staff engineer in a printing plant, I received upon my desk a petition which had been signed by all of the operators of the Monotype keyboard department. The petition alleged that the time standards by which each operator's productivity was measured were unfair. It asked that the time allowances be increased in order that the workers could make extra compensation under the existing wage incentive plan. My purpose in presenting this incident is in no sense technical but some understanding of technical factors is necessary for the sake of clear exposition.

The Monotype keyboards operated by these people are machines akin to typewriters in the arrangement of letters for "touch system" fingering, but there are many more keys and, on some occasions, as many as seven alphabets, instead of only two as on standard typewriters.

On the Monotype the depression of a key does not produce a visible letter as a typewriter does, but merely perforates a moving paper ribbon with coded signals which represent the individual characters. These perforated ribbons, when completed by the keyboard operators, are fed through the casting machines and there "play" the casters in much the same manner that paper ribbons actuate an old-fashioned player piano. The operation of the caster is of no concern to us here.

In addition to striking letter and space keys, operators are required to "justify" each line so that right as well as left margins will be uniform. They do this by utilizing a computing device which measures the space remaining or "shortage" of each line and divides this distance by the number of word spaces in the line. The operator can perceive what to do by reading a scale and then making two prescribed key strokes for positioning appropriate justifying wedges on the caster. These mechanical details are unimportant; it is only necessary to understand that keyboard operators rhythmically strike thousands of keys each day, with a pause for scale reading and justification at the end of each line.

Measurement of performance for such a task obviously must take cognizance of more than key strokes and lines. The degree of difficulty of the manuscripts being composed will, of course, be equally influential in enhancing or inhibiting output. Clear, double-spaced English text set to wide measure can be produced much more rapidly than an abstruse scientific paper, interlined by the author's corrections, bristling with symbols, and set to narrow measure.

The standard used to measure the performance of these operators accounted for these factors by a scale of classifications, with "straight matter" as a base and ascending degrees of difficulty which could be accumulated or interpolated as demanded by the task in hand. The standard itself allowed 15.6 minutes for each thousand ems set. This measurement of ems set then was multiplied by the classification factor, unity for straight matter, 1.10 for narrow measure, 1.40 for tabular matter, and so on, to yield what were called "classified ems." The sum of classified ems set by each operator during each month became the operator's "credit" for the month. This figure, when multiplied by the standard time allowance of 15.6 minutes per thousand ems, gave total standard minutes earned during the month.

Efficiency, upon which the incentive increment was based, was then computed by dividing total standard minutes earned by total minutes worked upon these measured tasks. There was also a quality factor intended to inhibit errors but this need not concern us here. The equation to measure efficiency and determine incentive pay was essentially

$$E = \frac{15.6\,MC}{T}$$

where E = Efficiency,
     M = Ems set, in thousands,
     C = Classification factor,
     T = Minutes spent on measured work.

The standards in dispute had been set in 1912, some thirty-five years earlier, by a man who later became Professor of Mathematics at Massachusetts Institute of Technology. This rather curious circumstance had nothing to do with the validity of the system of measurement, of course, but the fact remains that the standards had been satisfactory—at least they had been accepted by the operators without protest—for a long time. If longevity is a test of time study validity, then these standards were valid; indeed, there was no apparent reason to think otherwise.

The internal organization of the department at the time of the protest must be mentioned as relevant to the problem. Prior to and during World War II, all of the keyboard operators, with a single exception, were girls, each of whom knew touch system typing at the time of hiring. After the War a combination of public spirit and business expansion led to the hiring of a dozen or so male veterans, whose aptitudes for keyboarding were good but whose background training in typing had been somewhat variable. Some of these veteran trainees had been upgraded rapidly from "straight matter operators" to "tabular operators" to "all around operators" in order to meet expanded production needs.

Such was the situation at the time the letter of protest appeared upon my desk.

III

On the Administrative Process

THIS CASE HISTORY, like all of the many which are narrated in the literature of administration and management, is unique in itself; there is not nor ever will be any other case exactly like it. Yet it still may be used diagnostically to generalize; to comment upon attributes common to all kinds of administrative problems.

Again emphasizing the intent to establish general truths, it may be said, first, that the protest, that is the action requiring administrative attention, was socially and historically determined. The protest would not have been made at all fifty years ago and, if it had, the administrative action taken then would have been quite different from the administrative action taken now.

This first observation, it seems to me, is a matter of some importance. It means that administrators can influence the environments under their purview only to the extent that this influence is consonant with existing social mores. It also means, of course, that the problems which confront administrators will be determined to a very considerable extent by contemporary society. Fifty years ago, with more autocratic management the rule, the operators would have required much more provocation before daring to complain; fifty years ago management would have been much more likely to suppress a complaint, if the operators had dared then to make one.

2

In delivering the letter to a staff engineering executive, the keyboard operators had made their protest by a clear-cut violation of "proper" organization channels. The letter should have come through their line foreman, the superintendent, and the general manager. Engineering, if engaged at all, should have been assigned to the task by the executive to whom this staff agency was attached.

Several speculations on this action are possible: (1) the keyboard operators followed what *they* thought was the proper organization channel; (2) the operators did not think about organization channels at all but only did what "came naturally"; (3) the operators consciously violated prescribed channels to avoid possible blockade by the foreman, sensing that he might feel criticized by their militance; (4) the operators consciously violated prescribed channels in order to reach one whom they believed would be sensitive and responsive to their complaint; (5) the engineer by his own behavior had perhaps encouraged such direct communication and had in this regard encroached upon the line foreman's authority; etc.

Of these speculations (1) and (2) probably come closest to the mark but all are important and will be dealt with in later chapters. It will suffice now to state a general truth: tables of organization are seldom quite what they seem to be, and they do not often mean the same thing to the administrator that they do to the rank and file.

3

Decision and action were necessary. The keyboard operators had expressed their convictions that the standard was unfair. To ignore the protest, that is, seemingly to do nothing, would not have been inaction or indecision at all but, on the contrary, action and decision of the most militant kind. Indeed, inaction would have been equivalent to suppression, or at least attempted suppression, of the operators' protest.

In every such case the same kinds of decision choices are before the administrator: (1) he may decide to take some kind of action; (2) he may decide to do nothing, that is, make a null decision; (3) he may be indecisive. I have already pointed out that (2) and (3) do not maintain the status quo and now want to add that they are *not the same*. Both result in no action on the matter in hand but the decision not to act—often the very best decision which can be made—*is* a decision, an act of will and volition, whereas indecision is a kind of administrative failure, an expression of vacilation and indecision.

Both result in no action but they are not the same because the difference between decision and indecision is perceptible, it cannot be concealed. A decision to do nothing may bring resistance and protest; indecision will also bring contempt.

4

In addition to the evident necessity for making a decision, explaining away or rationalizing the complaint would be futile, despite the fact that "logic" supported the accuracy of the standard. After all, the standard had proved to be an acceptable and fair measure for thirty-five years, why then had it suddenly become too stringent? Moreover, some present operators, all of whom had signed the complaint, prospered under the standard; if they could, why was the standard not fair to all?

Then too, these understandable arguments could be given statistical and mathematical support: all of the variables in the situation remained unchanged, except the important one of ems produced. The operators worked the same number of hours each day, classifications were specified by the same rules interpreted by the same people, and the allowance per thousand ems was just the same as it had been for years. Such variability as might exist from page to page and line to line of copy, and differences in judgment of classification would be compensating over the very large number of characters struck.

Thus, it could be argued, efficiency was down simply because the operators did not produce enough to earn the extra pay that the incentive plan provided. They did not receive extra compensation simply because they did not deserve to, and this was *their* fault and not the fault of the standard.

A decision to meet the protest in this way would be the likely response in all too many cases; we are all trained—indeed overtrained—to be logical and we all react to justify ourselves when confronted with the imputation of error. Management, having caused the standard to be set, has become sponsor to its accuracy; to admit even the possibility of unfairness is to admit error and fallibility. This is bad enough when logic is against you. When logic is on your side, the admission becomes unthinkable.

And so the decision is made, by logic and self-justification, to deny that the standard is unfair by "proving" its fairness to the operators. Such an attempt is futile, because proof in such a case is impossible. The operators do not petition that the standard is unfair because they have *proved* it so, they petition because of what they *believe*, and such beliefs as theirs are not to be refuted by logic.

In saying this I am quite aware that the operators feel just as logical as management and are similarly motivated by training and instinct. To them, failure to earn bonus constitutes "proof" of unfairness. This belief cannot be shaken by counter "proofs." It may be logical and it may be natural to try but it also is futile.

5

In passing, I cannot resist citing an analogous case, in an altogether different sphere, to support these statements.

I once heard a former military attaché to the American Embassy in Moscow, Vice-Admiral Leslie C. Stevens, discuss his experiences informally before a group of faculty colleagues. Admiral Stevens was at once gracious and intelligent and had read widely and deeply about the communists, their ideology, and their strategy of conquest.

He made the point that the communism of Stalin and his cohorts rested upon a foundation of logic and suggested that a demonstration of error in this logical foundation might lead eventually to collapse of the whole structure. The suggestion was advanced that the biological fallacies of Lysenko could be the target of such an attack and it was agreed by the scientists present that this part of the edifice could be exposed as logically unsound.

However, a psychologist who was present asked this question: "How many followers of communism are loyal for logical reasons and how many adhere to the cause from emotional attachment?" He ventured to guess that were very few of the first and a great many of the second and followed by making this key point: the few who were communists because of logical considerations might become disaffected upon demonstration of fallacy, but the many who simply "believed in" communism would become more strongly attached than ever by outside attacks upon their "logic."

The analogy, of course, is clear. We "prove" communism to be "wrong" just as we might "prove" the petition of the keyboard operators to be "wrong." In both cases we may logically "win" our point. But unfortunately we do not win at all. We may gain an inch with the few logicians but we lose an ell with all the others.

In advancing these arguments I am, by my own reasoning, trying to convince you, the reader. If your beliefs run counter to mine and I fail to convince you, I shall have added support for my argument. On the other hand, if by logic I do convince you, I shall have refuted my own case, This seeming paradox must await explanation by a better philosopher than I.

6

To the necessity for making a decision and the futility of logical refutation may be added other attributes of the administrative process and some of these, it seems to me, can be stated well by contrasting the role of the administrator with that of the scientist in the laboratory.

Part of this contrast already has been made, at least by inference, because the scientist is bound by logic and reason above all else. He may turn his researches in a given direction because intuition suggests the more fruitful of alternate paths (indeed this could be described as an administrative decision) but once embarked upon experiment, logic and reason must be dominant.

Then too, the experimentalist is not beset by the same compulsion to decide as the administrator. Let an experiment fizzle or yield a dubious result and it may be repeated or modified again and again until the rigors of scientific accuracy are satisfied. This does not say that the scientist need never reach a conclusion but simply that his compulsions in this respect are not so pressing. The reasons for this relate to several interdependent factors.

The scientist's situation, one might say by definition, must be reproducible within very close limits; he must be capable of repeating the same carefully controlled experiments as often as need be for sound conclusions and, moreover, others elsewhere must be capable of doing the same thing by way of verification.

The administrator, of course, has no such facility at his command. He, perforce, must deal with people and for them events march in such a way that no moment or situation ever may be reproduced in its entirety. This is true in the laboratory too, if one considers the people there as well as the physical objects under study. They, the scientists and technicians, are not the same during Experiment No. 2 as they were during Experiment No. 1, and sometimes due account must be taken of this, if scientific rigor is to be maintained. But, nonetheless, the objective of their work, the experiment itself, may be reproduced.

There is another facet of this which can be mentioned, although the point may be strained in the making. Let an administrator err, or put his foot in his mouth, or unjustly castigate an employee, and he sometimes cannot recapture the ground lost by his mistake. He may correct himself or he may apologize but the vestiges of the blunder or the harshness will remain.

This notion of administrative "irreversibility" was conceived quite suddenly years ago, when an executive rebuked a subordinate in my presence. The young man in question had been a machine operator on shift work and he had been paid a differential for rotating at four-week intervals between each of three shifts. To fill a vacancy in an office department, he was promoted, without increase in salary but with the privilege of working all day-work. There were, of course, other desirable attributes in the change: the office job implied higher status and greater opportunity for advancement than tending a machine, and the young man was understandably enthusiastic about his prospects.

Under these circumstances he was called into the office of an executive for some minor detail relating to the transfer. The boss, it so happened, endured chronic difficulties arising from multi-shift operation of the plant. Employees did not want night work and problems repeatedly arose about the issue. In this case the executive could see only that this was another shift worker escaping to daytime hours. He addressed the young man very severely, telling him that he should be made to work shifts in the office or, alternately, lose the shift increment to his salary as a kind of payment for the privilege of working in the daytime.

The incident itself was trivial and I remember it only because of one dramatic quality: the new job, which had been so enthusiastically anticipated by the employee, at once became a mouthful of ashes to him. Concerning the point here, could the executive have "reversed" the situation, even by apology? Clearly, the answer is no. The spirit induced by the promotion had been crushed; it could be raised again by appropriate action, but only partially, not to its former high level.

7

Other, much more dramatic examples, of the irrevokable nature of some administrative decisions can be cited.

During the early days of World War II a large company was offered government contracts for military goods and was thereby required to certify compliance with the provisions of the Walsh-Healy Act. Among these is a requirement that there shall be no discrimination with respect to race, color, or creed.

In this plant, located in a border state, locker rooms, toilet facilities, and cafeterias were separate for white and colored workers. Had they been left so, no trouble would have occurred—at least not then—nor would the government have invoked the letter of the law to compel integration, since they were then agreeable to existing separate facilities in the same region. There was, in short, no problem.

However, the manger of the plant himself decided— long before the famous Supreme Court decision negating the separate but equal doctrine—that segregated facilities were discriminatory and in violation of the Act. He had the partitions removed and his troubles began—irrevocably. The white workers went on strike in protest, demanding that segregated facilities be restored. But if that were done, discrimination would be inevitable, the act of restoration itself would be discriminatory and in violation of the law. Moreover, had the partitions been restored, negro workers undoubtedly would have gone on strike themselves, a situation equally bad.

The decision, as I have said, was irrevocable and the strike was resolved only by seizure of the plant by the government. It was then against the law to strike against the government, so the striking workers were compelled to return to the integrated plant or lose their jobs. Time and social change have solved the problem and integration is now the accepted way of life in this plant.

The notorious Little Rock, Arkansas, incident is of exactly the same kind. Here the local School Board had decided upon limited integration in one school. Governor Faubus, declaring that violence would take place if the nine negroes attended Central High School, called out the National Guard to prevent the negroes from entering the school. His action was irrevocable. Take away the troops, as he did when so ordered by the Federal Court, and violence was inevitable, the Governor himself had practically invited it. Leave the troops to prevent the integration proposed by the local School Board itself, and the negroes would have been up in arms, to say nothing of Federal law enforcement. The only possible solution was that taken by President Eisenhower, to enforce the law by force of arms. Only time and social change can resolve the now continuing conflict and force must be maintained until that happens. Sentiments on integration are beside the point in these examples; they are intended only to illustrate the irreversible, irrevocable character of some administrative decisions.

8

The requirement of reproducibility in the laboratory carries with it two implications which also are lacking in the administrative process. The scientist is in control of the variables which affect his experiments and he usually can give them quantitative expression. The administrator often is unaware of the significant variables in the problems and situations which confront him and, even when he knows what they are, he often can neither control nor measure them.

How, for example, could one assess the emotional content of the keyboard protest? To what extent did the operators find motivation to complain among themselves, from home environments, from military experience, from executive dominance, from childhood, from the history of labor-management relations? No one knows, neither the operators themselves, nor those in management.

These arguments are applicable to results as well. Scientific experiments are "solved" and the results are quantified. Administrative problems in a very real sense have no solutions and there are no absolutes in the measurement of executive performance. Handsome profit can come from poor as well as good administration and loss can be incurred despite the best of direction. The church mortgage can be burned despite, as well as because of, good management. Military victory can come to the bungler and defeat to his opponent, who may be tactically and strategically, i.e., administratively, superior. We cannot measure administrative results other than relatively, although we are all prone to accept such measurements as are made as absolute.

Of what moment is it to dwell upon these very obvious things? Most, indeed the vast majority of decisions are easy to make, the course of action clear. It is not often necessary to search for hidden factors, to weigh and assess and weigh again. If this were not so, we should all go mad from the plethora of decisions thrust upon us as individuals and as members of organizations.

This is true, most decisions are easy and most results not critical. But, infrequent as they may be, there *are* difficult decisions to be made and critical results to evaluate, and it is here that the administrator stands or falls.

These considerations are important only because they may contribute to understanding. Administrators behave in countless situations as though indecision were not decision; they seek to be logical and find only rationalization; they quantify and then use the numbers not only beyond the limits of their accuracy but also as though the numbers expressed all the variables; they sometimes proceed recklessly, as though their steps could be retraced; they are overly satisfied when results are good and overly repentant when they are bad.

IV

On the Administrative Process

ACTION

ALL OF the arguments for which the keyboard example was presented have been made but the interested reader may be wondering what happened, what decisions were made, what results achieved. It is only fair to reveal the happy ending to the affair.

The first action taken was to route the petition through the appropriate channels of organization. The petition was personally returned to the spokesman for the operators with the request that he submit it to his foreman. Assurance was given that this was not merely evasion, that the protest would not be ignored, and the foreman and superintendent were apprised of these actions. Thereupon the petition did go through appropriate channels and, in a meeting of management people, assignment was made to the engineering group.

It is important to say that these preliminaries were marked by strong emphasis upon responsiveness; there was no attempt to deny the allegations of the petition, no suggestion of resentment at the operators militance. Nor was there any corresponding suggestion of appeasement; the operators were not told that everything was going to be all right, nor that their demands would be met. They were told only that there would be thorough and objective investigation and they were told this in the forthright, equable manner that I have characterized as responsive.

Here the word responsive connotes something more than an *outwardly* agreeable manner; it also means that the respondent *in his own mind* is sincerely seeking an objective and equitable solution and is not merely trying to "buy off" the complainants with honeyed words. This is important ethically and also practically if one believes, as I do, that lack of sincerity will be perceived and suspected, a point which already has been made with respect to null decisions versus indecision.

These initial and preliminary actions were followed by meetings with each of the three shifts of operators. By deliberate intent management representation was limited to three: the foreman, the personnel director, and the engineering investigator, in the hope that this would encourage operators to express their views freely. Despite this and despite the kind of atmosphere described, the first meeting required a patient hour before the operators began to talk. Their revelations were worth waiting for.

The most dramatic and by far the most fruitful disclosure related to the scheduling of work on each machine. The workers alleged that each day was characterized by a succession of machine changes, from one type size to another, from one type face to another, and from one arrangement to another, all beyond that to which they were accustomed and all without allowances in the time standard.

Inquiry of the scheduling group quickly revealed that this was true. They, the schedulers, were under heavy pressure from sales people and customers and had responded to that pressure by doing less work on more jobs, in the understandable hope that this spreading of effort would keep everyone reasonably satisfied. The consequences of this were much more than operator dissatisfaction with machine changes: the rate of turnover of work had been diminished, more storage facilities and floor space were required, funds for working capital were frozen in work-in-process, and production control difficulties were compounded by the increased number of items in process. These forces had been felt independently but it was the protest and meeting of the keyboard operators which revealed the cause.

Corrective measures promptly were introduced. More work on fewer jobs not only would have a beneficial effect upon the operators by increasing their incentive opportunity but also would benefit management in simplified production control, additional floor space, and diminished working capital requirements. This is a major point: by avoiding the age-old technique of attempted suppression, the conflict arising from the petition has yielded positive gains to *both* parties in dispute.

Making a conflict yield positive gains to both disputants has been called *integration* by Mary Parker Follett,[1] as opposed to domination or compromise, and more will be said about this important concept later. At the moment it will suffice to note that the contribution of integration to the keyboard situation has been practical, as stated just above, and psychological as well, in that the keyboard operators could and did feel gratified at this beneficial result of their militance.

Revelation of deterioration of scheduling procedure was paralleled by comparable disclosures on machine maintenance. During the war customary machine servicing necessarily had been curtailed because of manpower scarcity, and the pre-war rebuilding program had not been resumed. Operators claimed that their machines would run only to

[1] Henry C. Metcalf and L. Urwick (Eds.), *Dynamic Administration, The Collected Papers of Mary Parker Follett.* New York, Harper Brothers, 1940.

the accompaniment of frequent interruptions, each minor in itself but particularly harassing to the rhythmic task of keyboarding.

Again, possession of the knowledge could and did lead to a mutually profitable result. A one-by-one machine rebuilding program was begun and again both practical and psychological benefits were realized.

2

These things were important, of course; they affected the operators' productivity and earnings but they did not get to the heart of their petition. To test the validity of the standard it was agreed that a series of production studies would be made, with the results of these computed and posted for all to see. Much emphasis was placed by management upon the objectivity of these projected studies; stop-watch data would be taken and results revealed on a let-the-chips-fall-where-they-may basis, regardless of whether the results supported or negated the validity of the standard.

This part of the affair almost came a-cropper in a way which jeopardized not only evaluation of the standard but personnel relations as well.

Assignment for the agreed upon production studies was made to a member of the engineering staff who had done a good deal of work previously upon keyboard problems. It was believed that he enjoyed the confidence of the operators and that he clearly understood the requirements of the task. Such was not the case.

After some days, the observer produced a few efficiency figures, all of which were so high as to indicate that the standard was quite attainable. These were posted upon the department bulletin board as agreed. Posting promptly brought vigorous protest from the operators.

Efficiency figures are, of course, ratios and all ratios should be suspected until the quantities comprising numerator and denominator are known. In these cases numerators and denominators should have been large, that is, each production study should have been sufficiently protracted to insure a fair cross-section of the day's work, in order to encompass all of the kinds of things which break the rhythm of production. Unfortunately, this kind of observation had not been made. Instead, the efficiencies posted had been derived from observation of only a few lines of composition over intervals of from five to seven minutes.

The antagonistic reaction of the workers to this kind of information is easy to understand. To them, all of management's protestations of objectivity were so much propaganda. To them, management was behaving in the age-old way, preaching honesty and practising deceit. In just such situations are the suspicions and animosities of labor-management history felt.

To abate at least a measure of the hostility generated by this seemingly overt act the production study program was at once turned over to the operators themselves. The original observer was withdrawn with appropriate apologies for his actions, selected operators (the shift supervisors) were supplied with a stop-watch, and instructions were given in its use.

This had quick and beneficial results. Observations by the supervisors upon their fellow workers led to their reporting upon the inadequacy of training, a circumstance which has been remarked upon previously. In customary job progression an operator would become skilled and productive upon "straight matter" before promotion to "tabular," and skilled in that status before promotion to "all around operator." This pattern had been upset by post-war production demands and there were some in tabular and all around classifications who scarcely had acquired skill for the rapid composition of straight matter. It was understandable that they could not attain the standard for which their experience was far too limited.

To resolve this problem, the operators themselves proposed a rotating training program: each short-service operator would be assigned only work commensurate with his ability for a period of several weeks, during which instruction would be given and measurement of performance made. This measurement then would determine incentive pay for an ensuing period, after which the operator would be "on his own."

Additional details relating to other facets of the problem could be given but it is enough to say that this proposal worked well. Assignment to work of less difficulty brought high performance and this level of attainment held upon reassignment to more complex copy. Within a few months the case was closed; there was no change in the standard, nor has there been protest since.

3

A friend who read these pages remarked that this case was badly chosen, that there should have been a labor union to complicate the picture. While it is quite true that the presence of a union would have altered and complicated the case, to say this is to miss the point, for the narrative is quite subordinate to the analysis. Regardless of the case chosen, whether a union is a part of the problem or not, whether the problem is industrial, academic, military, or political, these things may be said once more:

Administration is as yet an art, refined in the clinic of

experience and subject as well to the native aptitudes of its practitioners. The framework of the administrative environment is in part determined by society, which governs the kinds of problems which arise and the kinds of action which may be taken.

However, at any time and in any society, these problems, of whatsoever kind they may be, demand decisions in such a way that deferment often is not possible; no decision at all often is equivalent to militant action.

In seeking to make "correct" decisions, administrators are prone to rely unduly upon logic and this frequently is futile. Problems arising from beliefs, even when the beliefs are quite fallacious, are not to be resolved by logical explanation.

To these characteristics may be added those which have been described by contrast: the non-reproducible nature of administrative situations, coupled with the impossibility of reversing a blunder; the inability of the administrator to control the forces at work, or even to identify all of them; the difficulty—often the practical impossibility—of quantification; and the absence of any but relative measures of results. These attributes are common to administrative situations everywhere.

V

On Organization

A FEW YEARS ago, at a lecture on public health administration,[1] I had the good fortune to hear a case history of organization which I shall repeat here for the purpose of analysis, in the manner of the keyboard situation described previously. Again, it must be emphasized that this case has not been chosen because of its uniqueness but because of general conclusions to be drawn from it.

The accompanying diagram is a conventional organization chart of the diagnostic x-ray department of a large hospital, to which some fictitious names have been added for convenience. The technical stem of the organization is under the direction of Mr. Adams and the professional or medical stem is under the direction of Dr. Jenkins. Adams has Mr. Beebe as a line assistant in direct charge of the department and several other staff aides, of whom only Smith, the personnel officer, is relevant to this discussion.

Under Beebe is Miss Daniels, as manager of the department, and she in turn supervises file clerks, dark room attendants, transcription clerks, an appointment secretary, and Miss Edwards, the chief x-ray technician, who, according to the table of organization, has under her direction seven technicians engaged in taking the diagnostic pictures.

The prescribed operating routine would, of course, begin with assignment of patients by their doctors for the x-ray

---

[1] Given by Mr. James Tower of Industrial Relations Counsellors. The narrative of the case is as I have recalled it and has not been reviewed by Mr. Tower.

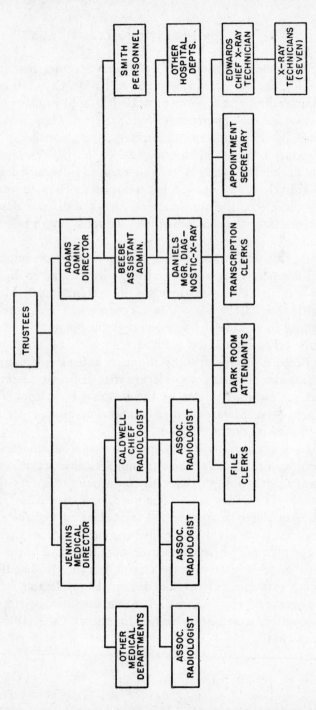

Fig. 1. Hospital organization chart.

pictures deemed necessary for diagnosis. Specifications for the taking of these would be prepared by Dr. Caldwell or, again according to the table of organization, by one of his three associates. Appointments with patients then would be made by the appointment secretary, the prescribed pictures would be taken by one of the technicians, developed by the dark room attendants, and read and diagnosed by Dr. Caldwell or by one of his associates. They in turn would dictate to the transcription clerks and, after diagnostic use, the x-rays and histories would come to rest at the hands of the file clerks.

While this was the prescribed routine, there were important differences in actual operation, which came to light when a crisis developed through the resignation of Miss Edwards. Mr. Beebe met—in fact, compounded—this crisis by issuing an extraordinary order: that the number of x-ray pictures taken should be reduced forthwith by forty per cent. Beebe gave this order without consulting Adams and with singular disregard, considering that he was a hospital executive, for the welfare of the hospital's patients. He also paid Miss Edwards a nice compliment by the magnitude of the specified reduction.

There was naturally a very great uproar from the medical people at this precipitate and impracticable action, and the trustees felt obliged to retain consultants to survey the situation. The consultants soon perceived that Miss Edwards was indeed a capable and important part of the organization. Not only did she supervise the technicians who took the pictures (there were never more than four of these, despite the seven shown on the chart), but she also handled appointments with patients and exercised considerable leadership over the clerks and dark room attendants who, it will be noted, were not under her direction on the table of organization.

Just as Miss Edwards had fewer assistants than specified, so also did Dr. Caldwell. The three associate radiologists were non-existent; Dr. Caldwell did all the work himself. His procedure was unusual. I have been told that a radiologist in such a position should have considerable contact with patients, in company with their physicians, for the purpose of making good decisions about the x-ray pictures to be taken. Dr. Caldwell never saw any patients either in the clinic or at bedside.

Even more it would be expected that Dr. Caldwell would give professional guidance to Miss Edwards and her technicians and to the dark room attendants, counselling them about optimum positions for the patients, exposure times, developments that were good and those that were obscure, all the subtleties that would enhance the diagnostic process.

Dr. Caldwell did none of this except by written specification. He sat in his office all day long and wrote instructions for pictures to be taken and dictated diagnoses from those which had been taken and developed. When a set of pictures could not be read for diagnosis, Dr. Caldwell did not personally instruct the x-ray group, he merely ordered another set of pictures with revised specifications. And, if that set proved inadequate too, he ordered a third and a fourth. Corollary to this tendency was his invariable practice of ordering a lot of pictures each time, just to enhance the probability of getting what he wanted. In the sense that pictures were wasted by the hundred, Beebe's rash order was on the mark.

Caldwell's isolationist tendencies had other, more or less hidden effects. Patients were trundled to and from the x-ray department at what must have been mystifying and costly frequency and more than one of them must have believed himself more seriously ill than he actually was on this account. Organizationally, the technicians, dark room attendants, and Miss Edwards herself had their work robbed of satisfaction and understanding by Caldwell's methods. They never knew whether they were doing well or badly but had only mechanical roles to fill. The patients who came before their cameras were transformed from fellow human beings into raw material to be processed according to written specifications and, if need be, to be reprocessed again and again. The attributes of diagnosis and healing, naturally inherent in the situation, were taken away by the remote and impersonal behavior of the chief radiologist.

However, Dr. Caldwell was not incapable of a personal relationship of another kind. The consultants learned that his wife formerly held the position now occupied by Miss Daniels. One could have surmised that he received advice at home, with Mrs. Caldwell as a kind of sub rosa member of the organization, but this would have been sheer speculation; there was no evidence of interference at home. Much more interesting was a mild clandestine romance between the Doctor and Miss Daniels. Thus a channel of oral communication between the chief radiologist and the x-ray department did exist but the transmittal of information hardly could be called organizational, especially since Miss Daniels was found to give the operating group little or no active direction.

During the course of these developments, until Beebe issued his unfortunate order and a storm arose, Mr. Adams remained aloof. The consultants came to perceive that he did this by deliberate intent in the belief that an administrator must be kept free of detail in order that he may have time to "administer." Apparently Mr. Adams believed this absolutely, delegating the whole works to Beebe and having little or no communication with him. Thus, Beebe's order to reduce the number of x-rays taken, although badly conceived, was issued in conformance with conventional organization practice. If Beebe's action was presumptuous and rash for a subordinate, it was made so by the inaccessibility of the superior.

On the medical side Dr. Jenkins equally was aloof from the chief radiologist and from other medical staffs as well. However, this was a different kind of administrative abstention from that practised by Adams. Jenkins was an amiable elderly gentleman who let the medical departments go their own ways more for the sake of his own tranquillity than because of any deliberate, thought-about policy. And he was, no doubt, influenced by other factors which will be explored presently.

One final point will complete the narrative. In most organizations it would be expected that Smith, the personnel officer, would be among the first to know of employment needs. It also would be customary to rely upon such a person for advice concerning personnel policies and problems relating to them. Throughout all of the turmoil associated with Miss Edwards' resignation and Mr. Beebe's order no one sought assistance or counsel from Smith and he apparently either was oblivious to the problem or felt that it did not concern him. No doubt he did have duties relating to personnel matters but what these were is not known.

2

Conventional literature on organization describes three kinds of organization relationship: line, staff, and functional. It is usually implied that these relationships are clearly separable, stereotyped in behavior, and mutually exclusive. A line executive or supervisor is attached to the principal or operating stem of the organization and has direct and broad authority over his subordinates. A staff man is expert in some special field but has no authority over the parent line organization, being content, according to the folk-lore of organization, merely to advise the line executive to whom he is attached. (A staff executive has authority over his own subordinates, of course, but these are *his* line organization; he is supposed only to advise the main stem.) A functional executive is like the staff man in that he is expert in some special way but, unlike the staff man, he is supposed to be authoritative over the domain of his specialty. Associated with these conventions is the not infrequent belief that organization charts are accurate and indispensable maps of these relationships, with the various interconnecting lines showing the channels of communication and the arrangement of boxes establishing the hierarchy of organization.

That much of this is wishful thinking and over-simplification is well known. Organizations do not behave in the manner portrayed by charts nor are organization relationships simple enough to be described by one or the other of the three conventional terms. Charts and line, staff, and functional characterizations are useful but they are much less definitive, informative, and controlling than is commonly believed.

The chart, or portion of one, that is portrayed here does tell something about the organization—that is why it has been used—but there is much that it fails to convey. The inaccessibility of Adams is in no way suggested by the chart, nor is the attendant autonomy of Beebe. The connection between Daniels and Caldwell, while quite unofficial, is nevertheless an important part of the "real" organization. Assumptions drawn only from the chart about the role of Smith necessarily would be incorrect. Dr. Jenkins would be assumed to give at least some direction to Caldwell and to the heads of other medical departments. Miss Daniels' true supervisory role, or rather the lack of it, could be gleaned from the chart no more than her clandestine connection with the chief radiologist. And Miss Edwards would be looked upon as just another bottom-level supervisor instead of the key figure that she was.

These recitations may be answered by saying that the chart is supposed to portray what the organization ought to be, rather than what it is. From this point of view the diagram is much better. Still, it does not and cannot signify the proper role for Caldwell, who, in conventional terms, should have a line relationship with the associate radiologists (that is, if there were any), a staff relationship with the practising physicians whose patients he should see clinically, and functional authority over the x-ray technical people in matters concerning the x-rays themselves. Inability to portray the nuances of staff and functional relationships is a general weakness of organization charts which will be explored in a later chapter. At the moment it will suffice to emphasize that organization charts are not as good, or reliable, or effective as many administrators think.

3

In the narrative of the case, Adams was said to give no supervision to Beebe, and Jenkins none to Caldwell. Each had his own reason but the effect was the same: neither subordinate got supervised. Since each was a line officer, it is reasonable to say that this was wrong; each of these executives should have given direction to his subordinate.

Saying this gives no pause in the case of the Adams-Beebe-Daniels-Edwards chain of command. It is quite easy to imagine Adams giving an order to Beebe, Beebe an order to Daniels, and so on, and it is equally easy to imagine that obedience would be customary. But suppose that *Doctor* Jenkins orders *Doctor* Caldwell to see patients at bedside or to give active counsel to the x-ray technicians and dark room attendants. Such an order from one doctor to another would be most unlikely and, if given, would be very apt to receive a negative, rebellious response. If Dr. Jenkins wanted to effect these changes in Dr. Caldwell's conduct, he would know intuitively that any suggestion of command would be self-defeating.

This same point can be made in another way. Consider any three levels in a line hierarchy, that is, arrangements of three boxes in a vertical row, connected by lines to show the chains of command. Label these lieutenant-sergeant-private (any three consecutive titles would do just as well), the second general manager-superintendent-foreman, the third dean-department chairman-professor, the fourth buyer-assistant buyer-salesman, the fifth union local president-steward-member, and so on.

Between each of these—and many more like them—are marked differences in adjacent line relationships. The sergeant will not hesitate to be peremptory, indeed, according to legend, he is never otherwise; he will expect and will receive prompt obedience. The superintendent may be peremptory with his foreman and the foreman with his men, but this is less likely. The dean—I am one myself—had better not be peremptory at all, unless he wants an impolite and defiant response. And union officers, unless they have achieved an intrenched dictatorship, will recognize that their continuance in office is dependent upon the political support of their members, and they will couch their "orders" accordingly.

Some of these differences in executive behavior are individual, of course. No doubt there are rare sergeants who are less peremptory than assistant buyers and an occasional dean who is more commanding than a mild industrial superintendent. But in the main these generalizations hold and it is beyond the power and strength of executives to escape them. Designations of line, staff, and functional roles, and tables of organization are of much less consequence than the mores which govern organization behavior.

That these mores are shaped by necessity, environment, tradition does not lessen their power over the executive. Prompt obedience of peremptory orders in military organizations is regarded as essential to victory in battle and there are powerful sanctions to enforce this code in camp as well as in combat, during peace as well as in war. A military commander at any rank *must* give orders; to do otherwise would be to appear a misfit.

At the opposite extreme, in academic organizations, those in administrative positions *cannot* give orders. Behind this lies a long tradition of academic freedom, job tenure, diversification of scholarship and technical knowledge, and an absence of interdependence between branches of the organization. A dean who has been trained as a psychologist will have little success in attempting to be peremptory with a professor of mathematics. To try will reveal the weakness of the dean's position; he will have few and paltry sanctions for enforcement of his order (and no reward beyond personal good will); he will risk a charge of violating academic freedom, even when that issue is not involved; and he knows little about mathematics. This may have nothing whatever to do with the case either but will color the situation nonetheless. How can one trained in a science less profound understand and administer the affairs of mathematicians?

In just the same way each organization's code is formed. A labor union leader had best not forget that he is part of a crusade—the labor movement. In a department store the customer epitomizes the organization goal and shapes the executive's behavior; in a public utility, uninterrupted service is god; in a hospital, the needs of the patients dictate. The industrial foreman shares a common technical and social background with his men and is quite aware that other departments are dependent upon his for the regular flow of product, just as he is dependent upon others for his own operation. He cannot, however much he might want to, be as autonomous as the mathematics professor and the psychologist.

I have not, indeed cannot, do more than hint at the complex forces which create the mores of organization but I do want to mention one more: forces outside the organization which are exerted by society as a whole. Social customs change with time and, even when internal needs do not, organizations must perforce change with them.

This is easily exemplified. During World War II General Patton slapped a soldier for alleged malingering and was himself reprimanded for the act. Can one imagine that such a reprimand would have been the fate of any counterpart of Patton in 1812, 1863, 1898, or 1917? The answer is no, although for each successive date a reprimand to a general officer becomes a little more reasonable.

In industry a foreman can still be a petty tyrant sometimes. But large numbers of foremen now find any tendencies to tyrannize inhibited by the watchful eye of the shop steward and the latent power of the union behind him. This is internal, to be sure, but in non-union plants this same power is felt, only now it is fear of being organized, if one's own workers become sufficiently aroused. For that matter, the unions themselves came to their present power only when society as a whole became ready for their growth.

A history of transitions such as these would defy writing. Behind the reprimand to the General and the "mellowing" of the foreman lie Magna Carta, escape from feudalism, the industrial revolution, Eugene Debs and the Pullman strike, the Hawthorn Experiments, the New Deal, a multitude of people, events, ideas, and inventions. Let an officer contemplate violence or a foreman tyranny and each will be restrained by social forces as powerful as they are impalpable.

However, these pages are not concerned with history, but with administration. There is a widespread and erroneous belief that to be an administrator one must fill the image of the legendary "captain of industry," impressive and aggressive, decisive and peremptory. This is true only when to be impressive and aggressive, decisive and peremptory is appropriate to the organization to which the "captain" is attached. When this is not so, the result of such an attachment and such behavior is destructive either of the organization or of the executive.

The good administrator thus must be understanding and adaptive. He can direct his subordinates with continuing success and stability only by understanding the mores of his organization, by appreciating their power, and by conforming to their limits.

4

At some risk of anti-climax I should like to develop another theme. The organization deficiencies that have been described in the x-ray department of the hospital were revealed but not created by Miss Edwards' resignation and Mr. Beebe's order. Despite the continued existence of these weaknesses, this part of the hospital organization had functioned adequately in fulfillment of its primary purpose. Good x-ray pictures were taken, patients were correctly diagnosed, treated, and cured, and the department bore a good reputation throughout the city, the medical profession, and the rest of the hospital. It was an organization which succeeded, so to speak, in spite of itself.

This sort of thing—a substantial measure of accomplishment despite the most glaring organization faults—is as much the rule as it is the exception. Perhaps more. The observations which form this opinion necessarily have been limited but there is some substance to the notion. I have seen one industrial concern where the executive in charge of production had no grasp of the work ahead of his machines, beyond the jobs actually in process. I have seen the president of a small company give just as little direction to his subordinates as Adams gave to Beebe, or Jenkins to Caldwell. I have arbitrated grievances between a company and a union whose relationship appeared to be so fraught with enmity, lying, punitive discipline, and goldbricking as to insure, one would think, quick bankruptcy. I have seen one executive in a position of importance who would not make any difficult administrative decision (that is, in a positive way; his failure to act often was equivalent to default, as I have pointed out before) unless he literally was compelled to by the pressure of circumstances, or by the desperate importuning of his subordinates. I have seen bad intuitive decisions made repeatedly, while available quantitative information was brushed aside as irrelevant. And, at the opposite pole, I have seen numbers used as the basis for decision, when all the while the data supplied were deliberately falsified by subordinates in order to pacify the executive and preserve the status quo.

Yet all of these organizations have continued to exist

and some of them have flourished. A critical examination of *any* organization by an objective outsider would, I suspect, reveal comparable defects. This is hardly profound but still is worth saying to emphasize once more that there are no absolute criteria for organization success; each is weighed against others equally susceptible to error. As one very perceptive student remarked, organizations, in a certain sense, do not succeed by being better than their rivals but only by being "less worse." If effectiveness is defined as the fulfillment of organization purpose, without consideration of cost, and if efficiency is the ratio of fulfillment to the cost of attainment, then many, many organizations are effective and relatively few are efficient.

The point is worth making, too, because administrators are more than a little prone to be self-satisfied about their own organizations. Enterprises "succeed," that is, they are effective, therefore they must be skillfully administered; the top of the hierarchy must be doing a good job. *Post hoc, ergo propter hoc.*

This is not only faulty reasoning but dangerous administrative complacency; it is well constantly to be aware that success is relative, that such success as may be attained can come from an Edwards far down the table of organization, *in spite of* the Adamses, Beebes, and Caldwells who are at or near the top.

5

In making this plea for administrative awareness of fallibility, I have not answered a much more important and far more difficult question: what can be done about organization weakness, even when it is brought to light? More specifically, what can the administrator himself do to effect corrective action?

I have already said that what he can do is limited by organization mores and now add that he is not likely to effect improvement by drawing a new organization chart, as though changing the map would change the roads. Great faith is placed in "reorganization" as though it were a paper transaction, which, of course, it is not. These restrictions, however, do not leave the administrator bereft. Sometimes he can suggest corrective action or altered behavior, sometimes he can and will direct it, and sometimes he must punish or replace the recalcitrant subordinate. In each case he must make decisions in the manner previously described, invoking the rewards and sanctions available to him. In each case perception of organization is the first requirement.

To say that executives must make decisions "in the manner previously described" is hardly a prescription and may be cold comfort, but worse is yet to come. Suppose that the principal organization weakness is at the top? What then?

This was the case at the hospital and in most of the examples recited above. The indecisive administrator was a president, I will not say of what. The executives who relied upon falsified numbers were corporation presidents and so was their opposite who ignored numbers doggedly. The union-management conflict appeared to stem from determination on the part of top executives on each side, union and company, to spit in the other organization's eye.

In the hospital, trouble also stemmed from the top of the hierarchy. Dr. Caldwell is not likely to modify his conduct from any action taken by Dr. Jenkins, who not only is inhibited by professional restrictions, but also lacking in perception and initiative. To affect Caldwell, someone first must affect Jenkins and there is no one to do this except the Trustees. In the same way, Beebe's autonomy can be modified only by Adams and someone first must convince Adams of the error in his policy of isolation. Again, there is no one to do this but the Trustees and they are an inactive, "absentee" group, who can act only after crisis has brought disclosure.

In the preceding paragraph Jenkins and Adams have been described as "top executives" and then were said to be answerable to the hospital Trustees. This inconsistency can be clarified by saying that there is no ultimate "top" in any organization, for, in the last analysis, each administrator is answerable to someone, either a person or a group. In this sense there is no such thing as "total" autonomy but there are very great differences in degree. Let "top" be defined as an administrative level enjoying a high degree of autonomy, such that supervision and oversight of that level are relatively remote. This may be exemplified by conventional relationships between corporation presidents and boards of directors, college presidents and trustees, generals and admirals and the civil authority over them, political officials and the electorate, and so on. In the hospital Jenkins and Adams were "top" administrators in this sense and so, less conventionally, were Caldwell and Beebe, because each of their superiors had granted full autonomy, respectively by default and by deliberate isolation.

Perhaps this could be clarified graphically in organization charts by using short vertical connecting lines to signify close, intimate supervision and longer lines to separate adjacent levels having remote oversight. Vector fashion, the length of these lines could be directly proportional to the degree of lower level autonomy, but this is not a necessary refinement here, nor am I concerned about how long these "vectors" ought to be in any given situation.

A moment ago I asked what the administrator can do if he is perceptive of organization weakness. In the case of down-the-line deficiencies, where the administrative "distance" is short, this has been answered, not categorically and perhaps not satisfactorily, but answered none the less. When supervision is relatively close and executive perception keen, action can be continuous, independent of crises, and corrective rather than punitive.

However, this is not the case when top level people are themselves inadequate. Their organization connections with their superiors are remote, hence their administrative inadequacies will be revealed only by crisis and, when revelation does come by this dramatic means, displacement and replacement of the executive usually is the only feasible action. Presidents and generals who get into trouble seldom are subject to guidance and correction; they are fired, because, by the time their administrative errors are revealed, no other action is appropriate. I have never heard what action was taken by the hospital Trustees, after receiving the consultant's report, but it is a fair guess that Adams was fired and Jenkins kicked upstairs (there is a nice distinction here too). Beebe may have gone too but this is even more speculative; his fate may have been left to Adams's successor.

Beebe's case is, in fact, of unusual interest. Ordinarily, the "administrative distance" between the Trustees and Adams would be large, as it was, and that between Adams and his first assistant, Beebe, would be small. However, by his deliberate inaccessibility, Adams made the distance between him and Beebe large, so Beebe's misfortune came to light only with the crisis created by his rash order. If he was not fired for this transgression but preserved for the decision of Adams's successor, he could be retained then only by restricting his autonomy, and this would mean a shortening of the connection between him and his new boss.

Thus, what facetiously might be called "laws of autonomy" or "laws of administrative distance" are not restricted to the top or near-top of organization hierarchy but are applicable to any two adjacent levels:

1. When, by custom or intent, autonomy at the subordinate of two levels is limited and controlled, continuous correction of subordinate weakness, independent of crisis, is possible.

2. When, by custom or intent, autonomy at the subordinate of two levels is relatively great, revelation of subordinate deficiency will come only from crisis and corrective action will be limited, usually to replacement of the subordinate.

There is only one alternative to replacement in the second case and that is application of the first. Limitation and control of what has been a high degree of subordinate autonomy can lead to corrective action, but this is practicable only when lower echelon autonomy has been created by intention or default, rather than by convention. If custom requires autonomy, this alternative cannot be applied. A foreman who has been given much autonomy and who from its exercise has blundered into crisis may be retained and controlled by limitation and circumscription of the areas of his discretion. So also may a superintendent, or an instructor, or a Beebe. But this cannot happen to a president, or a general, or a managing director, or an Adams, or a Jenkins. For their organization roles autonomy is customary and for their inadequacy dismissal is the only answer.

6

This essay has been negative throughout: organization behavior does *not* conform to conventional line, staff, and functional notions; charts do *not* convey a complete or accurate picture of organization; the administrator does *not* act with freedom; organizations often are *not* efficient; corrective action is *not* prescribable. All of these *nots* may be unfortunate and even disillusioning but they seem necessary, if only to dispel prevailing erroneous beliefs.

Introspectively, these negatives probably also result from little to say about organization that is positive, a poor admission but the simple truth. It would be easy to suggest introduction of the vector concept into organization charts and the use as well of symbol notations to indicate the channels and the scope and kind of authority. But this, I think, would accomplish rather little. At the moment, the need does not appear to be more refined pictures of organization but understanding. Too many administrators—at least those who occupy administrative positions—cling to the belief that organization behavior is stereotyped. Too often the notion persists that the lines and boxes of a chart represent a reality that can be changed by rearrangement on paper. Some administrators buck the forces of custom and society, many more heed and obey them but are oblivious of their presence and power. And far too many in administrative positions complacently mistake tranquillity for effectiveness and effectiveness for efficiency.

VI

On the Delegation of Authority

AT THE moment when two people join in related or common purpose to form an organization, consideration must be given to division of the duties and responsibilities that are required to fulfill the organization's objectives. Let the lone barber on the neighborhood corner hire an assistant and questions of delegation must be answered. The assistant will cut hair, to be sure, but will he be permitted to use the cash register? May he extend credit to a customer when the boss is out? Or cash a customer's check? Or buy supplies? Or leave the shop to shave an invalid?

The answers to some of these questions will be understood in the nature of things, according to customs of the barbering trade. Other questions will be answered as events occur and still others by stipulation at the time of hiring. Thus the assistant comes to know what is expected of him and how much freedom he has in each kind of situation.

Questions of subordinate autonomy arise and must be answered in larger, more formal organizations in just the same way. Some of these questions will be answered by custom, some of them by organization needs, and some of them by direct instruction at the time of initial attachment. Other answers to questions of subordinate autonomy will be determined by the willingness or unwillingness of the superior to delegate authority to his subordinates. It is this last which concerns us here.

In the university organization with which I am familiar, custom and a considerable measure of deliberate intent have created and maintained a very high degree of local autonomy, with freedom for the exercise of independent judgment and action carrying all the way down to the students themselves. This very considerable degree of delegation not only has become a tradition in this particular organization but serves its needs as well: local autonomy is possible in a university in part because of lesser interdependence between organization units.

In other forms of organization, custom and need similarly help to determine local autonomy. Industrial organizations will exhibit many more restrictions upon subordinates than universities, and private universities are likely to have more lower-level decision making than those which are answerable to state legislatures. Military organizations will be different from any of these, in the direction of greater central control. Organizations to which people lend their services voluntarily necessarily must give subordinate volunteers greater freedom of action, lest they sever their attachments through dissatisfaction with overcontrol at the top.

Thus, the forces of custom and need largely shape the degree of local autonomy, the extent of delegation to subordinates. Moreover—and more to the point here—these forces are "acceptable" to superiors and subordinates alike because they are both customary and necessary. The soldier accepts the fact that his behavior will be restricted when he becomes a soldier; the civil servant knows that he will be bound by rules made by higher authority when he enters the civil service; the assistant professor knows that he will be accorded some freedom when he enters academic life.

But, beyond the effects upon delegation exerted by the

forces of custom and need, there is still that exerted by the individual superior in any superior-subordinate relationship. It is he, the superior, who accords to his subordinates greater or less freedom of action, within the boundaries created by custom and need. It is my belief that organizations suffer in this respect because superiors delegate less authority, less responsibility, and less freedom than they should for optimum results.

2

Executives do this, retain power in their own hands, for a number of reasons: they may lack subordinates sufficiently experienced or talented to be trusted with decisions; they may be fearful of subordinate error, for which they themselves may be held responsible; they may properly dread the drastic consequences which can come from touchy decisions, as, for example, in a labor-management affair. Apart from all this, and much more a determining factor, they may restrict their subordinate's authority, retaining it for themselves, because of their own psychological needs.

In saying that executives retain unto themselves more power than is optimum for organizational efficiency, and that they do this because of psychological need, I am far beyond my depth, for I have had no formal, and very little informal, training in either psychology or psychiatry. I have, however, observed many executives perform and, having conceived the idea, have looked for evidence and, indeed, have come to expect to find it. Those executives who do not appear to exhibit this "power-retention" or "power grabbing" propensity seem to me to represent the most skillful practitioners of the art of administration.

This business of looking for evidence is hardly exemplary of the scientific method, yet the notion rationalizes well.

All of us want to feel important, to others and to ourselves; all of us are impelled by drives—or whatever the right word is—which govern our behavior. More often than not, I suppose, these forces are so subtle as to be concealed from ourselves as well as from others, and we proceed to hold and to grab authority quite subconsciously.

Whatever the reasons, executives do retain more power than they should. By so doing they enhance their sense of importance, they strengthen their grip upon organization, they make their subordinates dependent upon them, they raise and maintain their status, and they compensate for their own inward insecurities. The big "I am" is a familiar figure in organizations everywhere; I am talking about the medium and little "I am" too.

If this is so, and I think it is, then a most important requirement of executive leadership is more subtle than the pronouncements of the Boy Scout Law: ". . . courteous, kind, obedient, cheerful, thrifty, brave, clean, and reverent." A good executive also should have that measure of self-confidence, status, achievement, stability, self-satisfaction, or whatever it should be called, that permits him to "let George do it," to the aggrandizement of George and the betterment of the organization.

This ability to subordinate self, to say "you decide," probably is contrary to ordinary human nature; everybody wants to boss everybody else from childhood up (parents, in fact, are probably the worst offenders). Yet, paradoxically, "letting George do it," saying "you decide" not only aggrandizes George, it does just the same thing for the superior who is wise enough to delegate. We fool only ourselves (admittedly this is important to each of us) when we hog the show. Delegation, on the other hand, not only releases valuable organization energy, it also raises the executive in the eyes of his associates.

3

Just as there are practical as well as emotional reasons inhibiting delegation, so there are practical as well as emotional consequences of power retention by executives.

One obvious characteristic of those who will not delegate is their eternal busyness; since they must decide everything themselves and since there are a great many things to be decided, they are always overburdened. This symptom usually appears with another, corollary one: great devotion to routine trivia, opening the daily mail, on the ground that the boss must know what is going on, minutely scanning daily production figures, initialling countless papers, approving, disapproving, reproving, in endless routine fashion. Long ago, during the depression, I knew a college president of this kind who would not even let a subordinate order small stickers reading "Please turn out the lights" until he, the president, had read the proof. Often, I think, executives of this stamp cling to these routines and clutch these prerogatives because they would not know what else to do and would feel bereft and insecure if deprived of routine.

A second practical effect of insufficient delegation is, of course, the blocking of subordinate development, which already has been stated in another way. By retaining power the executive makes the organization more dependent upon him and prevents the development of capable substitutes in the event of separation. Sometimes, in the case of small organizations where power is concentrated at the top, departure of the focus of that power, through death, illness, or separation, can destroy the organization, there being none left who can do aught but obey. In component units of larger organizations the effect is not so fatal but, even so, a measure of temporary chaos results when the source of all decisions leaves.

Dissatisfaction to subordinates is, of course, another paramount effect of too much centralized power. Not only is the opportunity to develop stultified but, in being continually told what to do, the subordinate is restricted in a way that can only be distasteful. While it is true that there are some persons who want neither freedom nor responsibility but prefer to be directed, such are not typical, and certainly are not representative of future organization leadership. To all who want to "get ahead," the boss who holds and pulls all the strings can only be a kind of tyrant.

Advocates of participation and team work as ingredients of organization success would do well to attend to delegation in this same connection. Like virtue and motherhood, everyone is in favor of team work and participation but too many mistakenly suppose that this means organization sponsored social activities, athletics, 25-year pins, and a gift at Christmas, plus, perhaps, that other virtue, "communication," wherein the boss is continually *telling* his subordinates what is going on. If participation is good for organization effectiveness and efficiency, as the Hawthorn Experiments have shown, then this good can come only from the genuine article, and this means decision making down the line to that degree permitted by custom and need. Because of restrictions placed by executives themselves, this is more delegation than that presently to be found in most organizations.

4

If an executive is motivated, perchance by reading these lines, to increase the autonomy of his subordinates, he must be on his guard against two things: rule-making and the punitive treatment of subordinate errors.

Superficially, it may seem possible to make rules without appearing to restrict local autonomy but, of course, this is not so; a rule may become impersonal with time but, impersonal or not, a rule is still a boss-made pronouncement which inhibits judgment at the local level even more than an oral order, a rule being rigid and lacking chance for give and take.

I remember an incident during the final months of World War II which gives this point dramatic emphasis. The Company for which I then worked had instituted the practice of paying regular wages for seven holidays. Being fearful of casual Monday or Friday absences when holidays fell on a Tuesday or Thursday, a rule was pronounced that no employee could receive holiday pay if absent either on the day before or the day after the holiday. It was stipulated that there should be no exceptions.

Shortly after this rule was made, July 4 fell on Sunday, which made Monday, July 5 a paid holiday.

During this time the invasion of Okinawa was under way and Japanese *kamikaze* pilots were giving our fleet a bad time. One of the Company's employees, who had given me training years before and of whom I was very fond, had two sons in the service; one of these boys had recently gone through the Iwo Jima fight unharmed and the other now was on a destroyer in Pacific waters.

Knowing of the father's anxiety, I had often stopped at his machine to ask after his boys and did so about two weeks after the July 5 holiday. He told me that his Navy son had been killed when a *kamikaze* had struck just at his battle station. The Navy Department telegram had reached the family on July 5, his wife had collapsed, and he had stayed at home on July 6.

His sorrow and distress at the loss of his son was apparent and understandable, and so was his extreme bitterness at the Company, for of course the no-exception rule was invoked and he got no pay for either July 5 or 6. To him, the organization that he had served for 35 years had behaved in a completely cold and miserly way at the most tragic moment in his life, a tragedy compounded by the drama of death in the cause of patriotism.

I immediately sought out the President of the Company and told him what had happened. He had not known of the rule—at least he was unaware of its rigidity—and was immediately sensitive to what had happened, leaving his office to go to the bereaved parent, to express sympathy for the loss of his son, and to promise restitution of the withheld pay—despite the rule.

Aside from the poignancy of the story, the point to be made lies in the atmosphère of governance by rule which had been created in the organization. In this case the man's foreman knew exactly what had happened to his subordinate, knew exactly what routinely would happen to his pay check, and could sense what the bitter reaction would be. Yet, knowing these things he took no action, made no recommendation for exception, because he was conditioned *by his superior* to obey rules blindly.

This same phenomenon in broader, even more rigid form appears as a consequence of some contracts between companies and labor unions and may be exemplified by reference to seniority clauses. Since seniority conflicts often are between workers rather than between workers and management, one might surmise that equity would be the dominant goal in each situation. Not so. The contract, i.e., the rule, says that action must follow the agreement to the letter, even when doing so works a gross and obvious inequity.

With a document as formal as a labor contract in being,

this attitude may be pardonable but then one discovers equal intractability toward any contract change giving freedom to the exercise of judgment within a framework of stated seniority principle. No, the contract has become dogma, sacred writ, an attribute of rules generally.

Seniority clauses illustrate another, futile aspect of rigid rule-making in human affairs. Seniority disputes, if equity is to be served, involve need for appraising differences between the employees involved: differences in length of service, skill, versatility, productivity, attendance, punctuality, compatibility, etc. When these differences are wide, decisions are easy and equity is served; when the differences are narrow, the rule will compel favor to a man with one additional day's service over another, even though the favored employee is less skilled, less versatile, a low producer, a habitual absentee, and completely incompatible with his mates. Aside from the fanciful mechanism of a differential equation—an impracticable solution, of course —there is no way to state such a rule in words and, at the same time, to serve equity in all the many-sided situations which are certain to arise.

In the environment of administration rules covering all possible contingencies are impossible to state. Attempts to write such rules will not only fail in their purpose but will violate equity and stultify delegation as well. A framework of rule within which subordinates are free to decide for themselves will serve the ends of sound delegation and abide by the old and sound adage, "the more law the less equity."

5

When a subordinate has been granted a measure of autonomy, he is sooner or later bound to make a bad decision, at least one that is so regarded by his superior. The conduct of the superior on such occasions will determine the decisiveness of the subordinate in the future.

This is not so obvious as it sounds. Every executive in every organization is accorded a certain range of authority. Those things about which the executive may make decisions may be stipulated in an organization manual ("In cases of infractions of discipline, the foreman shall have the power to discharge . . ."), they may be conveyed by verbal instructions ("I want you to do the buying in your department."), or they may be implied ("When a fire breaks out, call the fire department."). In any case, each executive at each level is supposed to have an array of things about which *he* can decide.

What I am concerned about is the succession of events which takes place all too frequently when the executive does decide a matter properly within his purview, but does so badly, in the eyes of his superior. What the higher executive does about his subordinates "bum decisions" has more to do with the preservation and cultivation of sound delegation than all the statements expressed or implied about local autonomy.

This too is not so obvious as it sounds. We have, in many organizations, deeply ingrained notions about "backing up" executives. Let a foreman unjustly discharge an employee and he will be "backed up" by making the discharge stick—but the foreman will be "chewed out" for his action. Let a buyer increase his stock by volume purchases when he should be buying short and the company will "back him up" by accepting the goods and paying the bills—but his boss will "blast" him as a stupid ass for his decision.

To do this may be natural and in some cases quite desirable but, more often than not, such dominantly punitive approaches to executive error serve only to relieve the choler of the boss and to destroy local autonomy. The manual still says that the foreman has power to discharge but, for the foreman who has been "chewed out," that power is gone; he will refrain from using this authority, even when he should. The buyer who was "blasted" for volume buying now will be a mouse in the market place, even though his boss still says that he retains the buying power.

To imply such drastic consequences of single incidents is to exaggerate, of course. But the effect is truly appraised, nonetheless; there *are* executives, many of them, who continually correct, redress, modify, change, alter their subordinates decisions in a punitive and finicky way that effectively robs them of autonomy. Often, perhaps always, these are the executives who need power for the satisfaction of their own egos; often these are the ones who set greatest store by "backing up" their people. Often these are the executives who complain about the indecisiveness of their subordinates when it is they themselves who are to blame. Thus, the punitive atmosphere that is created destroys autonomy while giving lip service to it.

Therapy for such a situation consists in changing the point of view from punishment to education. Now the foreman is reproved with the objective of having him make a good decision next time. Now the buyer is given economic understanding about the market, working capital, storage problems, and obsolescence, which will make him a better buyer, not a mouse.

The foreman merits another word. If he unjustly discharges an employee, is "chewed out," and "backed up," a costly inequity remains which cannot be removed by the punitive approach. The educational approach, at the opposite pole, does not certify removal of the inequity but does make it possible. If the foreman, in being educated, himself decides to restore the unjustly discharged employee to his job, equity is served, the conflict is integrated, and the foreman has become "a better man" in the process. Admittedly, this is a goal not easily achieved but only the educational approach permits even the possibility of attainment.

And it is only through this selfsame approach that sound delegation may be achieved and preserved.

6

Local autonomy and delegation of authority, it has been said in this chapter, are restricted beyond organization needs and mores, and beyond that degree which would be optimum. The causes of restriction have been stated as untrained personnel, fear of subordinate error, and, most of all, ego involvement on the part of superiors. This thesis has been advanced hesitantly, because of ignorance, yet with conviction derived from observation of executive behavior. From this conviction has come one specification for a good administrator: possession of that degree of self-confidence and security which does not require self-aggrandizement through the constant exercise of power.

The consequences of insufficient delegation are serious: dependence of the organization upon those who hold too much power; excessive burdens upon executives of this stamp, who often cling tenaciously to routine trivia; the blockade of subordinate development; and the depressing of subordinate morale through dissatisfaction.

These effects, at least insofar as they apply to subordinates, also can derive from excessive rule making and from the punitive treatment of what are deemed to be subordinate errors in decision making. Rules are just as stultifying to local autonomy as direct orders but are more rigid and hence more likely to lead astray and to violate equity. The punitive treatment of errors, applied too often or too severely, leads only to subordinate caution and indecisiveness.

All of this analysis says much the same thing: that very many executives are prone to hang on to too many decision making prerogatives, by day-to-day behavior, by rule making, by punishing subordinates who venture to decide. The cure is to find executives who are inwardly secure, to frame rules broadly and flexibly—and sparingly, and to use subordinates' errors to educate rather than to punish.

This is a good prescription but, like telling an alcoholic not to drink, one that is hard to follow. Still, some alcoholics do stop drinking when they come to understand the source of their compulsion. Perhaps, through this modicum of understanding, some executive may cease drinking at the fount of power.

VII

On Staff Organization[1]

MODERN organizations, as is well known to everyone, have been characterized by growth to large size. They also have been characterized—and this has been less often remarked—by the proliferation of staff elements. No doubt these developments have been interdependent to some degree.

The line executive in business and industry, who once figuratively "did everything," now is assisted by an impressive array of fiscal, personnel, legal, procurement, engineering, marketing, and research aides. The present day military commander leans upon his staff in planning, communications, topography, meteorology, supply, sanitation, medicine, and operations research to a degree unknown to his predecessors. The government official may have all these and statistics too.

2

According to the conventions of organization, the staff member is expert in areas such as these and is advisory to the line organization on matters appropriate to his expert knowledge. A staff man may not *tell* his line associates what to do; he may only *advise* them.

Toward organization superiors and peers, this convention holds well enough; staff people cannot boss those on

[1] This and the following chapter appeared in *Operations Research*, Vol. 4, No. 3, pp. 309–323. They are reprinted here by permission.

the same level or above them in the hierarchy simply because orders will not be accepted from equals or subordinates. Toward these levels of organization staff must give advice and this imposes upon them special problems, which will be examined later.

With respect to those below staff on the table of organization, the convention of an advisory relationship usually is violated. Toward these subordinate elements, staff tends to become functional in the manner defined on pages 33 and 34. Down the line its pronouncements are accepted as orders and not as advice.

The degree to which this functional relationship toward subordinates develops is dependent upon the amount and intimacy of staff communication with lower echelons. A fiscal officer, engaged in advising a board of directors or a chief executive on financial matters, is not likely to become functional because he has little contact with those to whom he can give orders, except, of course, for the subordinates in his own department. Similarly, a controller or a military planner will not violate the advisory convention because there is no need or opportunity to do so.

However, when a staff department does customarily deal with subordinate echelons, either as a convenience or necessity, the tendency toward a functional relationship does develop, with important consequences. This is readily exemplified by examination of the organization role of almost any personnel department in industry or business, a relationship that is graphically approximated in Fig. 2.

According to the conventional rules, the personnel department should deal with the line organization "through channels." Personnel problems requiring expert advice should go to the personnel department along the paths of communication established by the solid lines and advice

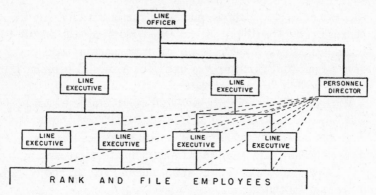

Fig. 2. Channels of communication in organization.

should flow back through this same conventional path. If the personnel director wishes to give advice, the rules say that he must do so through these selfsame channels, with orders as need be emanating from line executives.

This, of course, simply does not happen, not even in military or governmental organizations, where so much reverence is accorded to formal channels. Instead of the formal network, there actually exists a multiplicity of short cuts, a portion of which are shown by the dotted lines, and these are used all the time. They are used because they are direct and convenient, because they are necessary and efficient to avoid red tape, and because subordinate echelons do not understand the nuances of conventional organization and do what to them "comes naturally." This, incidentally, is precisely what the keyboard operators did with their petition (p. 10).

The use of direct communication means simply that subordinate line people have direct contact with higher echelon staff people on matters pertaining to personnel. When they do, they will receive advice, which will be couched variously, but however couched, will in all likelihood be accepted as orders. Let a foreman ask a personnel man how to handle the seniority problem of John Doe and he will be likely to accept the answer as a mandate, even when the intended advice goes contrary to the foreman's own opinion.

He will do this for fairly obvious reasons: because he went to the personnel man in perplexity, wanting to be told; because of a presumption of expertness on the part of the personnel man; and because the personnel manager is higher on the table of organization than the foreman. After all, would the company have put the personnel manager in that fine office with his own secretary and his name on the door, if he wasn't wise about personnel problems? One does not lightly flaunt expertness that is at the same time clothed with prestige and authority.

By this sequence of seeking advice, getting it, and having it tacitly accepted as instruction, the John Doe problem is settled. Since the personnel manager is likely to be more expert in personnel relations than the foreman, the proposed settlement of the case is likely to be a good one. What, then, is wrong if the staff man behaves in an authoritative manner or, conversely, if the subordinate line echelons accept authority from the staff?

The question is one of degree and extent. Let this process be repeated often enough and long enough and the personnel manager tends to become the foreman, or, more accurately, a number of foremen, if he has similar relations with other such line executives. He tends to become the foreman not for personnel matters alone but for other things as well.

This does not come about because the personnel manager steps in and begins to take over machine scheduling, or maintenance, or other technical matters; it comes about because the foreman himself is weakened bit by bit by encroachment upon decisions that should be his. John Doe has talked with the foreman about his problem and has perceived his indecision; he also sees that what finally is said comes from the foreman's mouth but is not a product of his mind or will. His dependence upon his foreman for the satisfaction of his wishes is now to some small extent transferred to the personnel manager. Let him next seek a better machine assignment, the kind of thing routinely handled by the foreman, and he will know how to go about getting it—by getting his demand to the ear of the personnel manager.

This has been exaggerated for effect but nevertheless contains much truth. I once knew a staff executive who studied the same keyboards discussed previously, in order to diminish errors and corrections while at the same time sustaining output. The investigation was a notable success technically but during its course the staff man, who was a trained psychologist, became the confidant of the operators and, when his research job was done, remained interested in their efficiencies, their error ratios, their wage rates, their promotions, and, indeed, everything about their welfare from marriages to births, deaths, and sickness. Let an operator want a day off or a different vacation period and she would go to the staff man, not to her foreman. The staff man, was closer to the throne and was moreover presumed expert in human relations. The foreman, until he finally became militant and demanded cessation of these end-run contacts, was reduced to the role of straw boss.

The psychologist, it may be added, lost his value as an investigator during this period, being fully occupied with keyboard department affairs.

The two effects, then, of staff tendencies to become functional with respect to lower organization echelons are the weakening of subordinate line executives and the loss of staff availability for their assigned missions. The first of these is obviously related closely to the problems of delegation discussed in Chapter VI. The staff expert who encroaches on the line by virtue of his rank and expertness has the same effect as the line superior who clutches all decision making to himself. Both, to the degree that they transgress, reduce the subordinate executive to the role of relay: he receives the message, amplifies it, and transmits it, but, having no say of his own, does not change it. By this means the line executive becomes habituated to advice and to indecision; by this means he loses some of the respect of his subordinates and some of his own self-respect as well.

In discussing the line executive who does not delegate authority, it was pointed out that busy occupation with trivia was characteristic of such a person. This too is somewhat analogous to the staff man who drifts into functional relationships with line subordinates. As staff, he is supposed to be advisory, not operational, within the boundaries of his expertness. If he grows into habits of operating the enterprise, even though his operating tendencies are confined to his expert knowledge, his value as staff adviser to his superiors is sharply diminished.

3

If it is agreed that such propensities should be checked and controlled, how and by whom shall this be done?

To begin at the bottom, it would be pleasant and desirable to have line subordinate executives who would militantly defend their decision making prerogatives, who would know that advice sought from the staff *was* advice, even though it came from an exalted staff vice-president or other high ranking executive. If this Utopia could be attained, then the case of John Doe would be settled by the foreman, not the personnel manager—and this would be so, even if the foreman followed the personnel manager's advice, *provided* he did so of his own volition.

Desirable as such a condition would be, it cannot be achieved unless staff itself behaves with restraint, and conscious restraint at that. When the personnel manager talks with the foreman, it is he, the personnel manager, who must be conscious of his rank and his expertness and the undue weight and authority which will be given to his words, unless they are voiced with care. His answer to the John Doe inquiry must be self effacing, with strong emphasis that it is given as advice.

To give this the added emphasis that it deserves, how shall the personnel manager respond when the foreman says, "What shall I do about John Doe's seniority?"

To be asked any question for information is, of course, subtly flattering because knowledge is implied. The personnel manager, therefore, is naturally inclined to reply, "Give Doe seniority above Smith." When he does, he will be guilty of encroachment. If he is just a bit wiser than this, he may use the subjunctive mood and say, "I would give Doe seniority above Smith." This carries a connotation of advice, to be sure, but the foreman still will be very likely to return to Doe and say, "The personnel manager says to give you seniority above Smith." This is not much better on the part of the personnel manager and is no better at all for the foreman-Doe relationship.

But now suppose the foreman says to the personnel manager, "What shall I do about John Doe's seniority?" and the personnel manager replies, "What do you think should be done?" This obviously puts the colloquy on an entirely different basis. If the foreman then says, "I'd put him below Smith on the seniority list," the personnel manager can find out why the foreman would so decide and can give his own reasons for a different view. If, in addition, the personnel manager emphasizes that the final decision is the foreman's, an altogether different organization result is achieved. Instead of an order, advice and information have been exchanged.

This kind of self effacing staff behavior must, of course, be consistent and repetitive. Good executives and sound relationships do not result from single incidents but accrue from a multitude of them. The decisive foreman will not become indecisive because the personnel manager tells him what to do about Doe, nor will the indecisive foreman become decisive by being encouraged to make up his own mind. But both will be affected to some slight degree, undesirably or desirably, by the personnel manager's behavior in each single case. And the cumulative effect of many such incidents will be profound.

Those who administer both staff and line can, of course, contribute to the establishment and maintenance of sound relationships by understanding the forces at work and by exercising influence toward their control. The main burden, however, must be borne by staff itself; it is they who must consciously suppress their natural inclinations to command in a way that is analogous to the precepts of sound delegation set forth previously.

4

Staff behavior toward organizational superiors and peers does not involve the problem of encroachment of authority but does present problems of equal importance: shall staff elements give advice *only* when asked and *only* on matters assigned by line superiors? Or shall staff, in addition, generate and proffer advice on matters it believes to be significant to the attainment of organization goals? In either case, lacking authority over superiors and peers, how shall staff have its advice accepted?

My own opinion on the first two questions is that staff which merely proffers advice when asked is not worth much, yet all too frequently this is the rule. The accountant or controller mills out numbers at specified intervals and feeds them to his line chief; the personnel manager rounds up recruits, interviews, hears grievances, advises about the new labor contract, and gathers statistics on industry and local wage rates; the medical department examines, treats, and records its case histories. The operations research group looks only at its direct assignments.

All of these things are necessary and desirable and it is wrong to say that they aren't worth much. They are—but they are worth much, much less than they could be if imagination and creativeness were part and parcel of the staff mission. The accountant or controller need not be a mere number mill, he can desirably create and shape policy by penetrating his numbers in ways imperceptible to his line superiors. The personnel man need not be merely the box into which personnel problems are dumped, he can be the astute diagnostician and therapist of the basic forces of conflict. The staff medical officer need not be only a practitioner, he can also contribute to public health, safety, and hygiene in ways that his line superior, lacking medical knowledge, could never see unaided. The operations analyst can perceive and examine broader and more fruitful fields with great benefit to his organization.

Granted that imagination and creativeness cannot be implanted in individuals who lack these qualities, what is

said here still is sound, because it urges the conscious removal of possible staff restraints. Establish a staff con-
trollership without granting it the freedom to imagine
and create and the result may be a mere plethora of routine
numbers, even though the controller is as imaginative as
anyone could wish. Charge this selfsame controller with
the exercise of imagination as a formal pact of his mission
and the result will be altogether different—and very much
better.

5

In either circumstance, sought for advice or created
advice, staff faces the problem of gaining line acceptance
from superiors and peers. Advice that is requested will be
accepted more readily, of course, but in any case salesman-
ship is necessary to successful staff achievement. Staff,
since they cannot give orders to superiors, must persuade.

Persuasion is, of course, an art about which one could
prate endlessly. There are, however, some attributes of the
art, particularly germane to staff organization, which may
be mentioned to good purpose.

First among these is the need for staff to recognize that
they will be obliged to persuade. This is not so silly as it
sounds; again and again staff people rush forth with
genuinely sound ideas in the manner of Jack Horner hold-
ing up his plum for all to see. The indifference which follows such bright-eyed presentation is then the cause of
much staff frustration, accompanied by damnation of the
stupid, reactionary line executives who are too obtuse to
know a bright idea when they see it. Realization that this
is the way of the cruel world not only can relieve frustration but lead to conscious planning of the strategy and tactics of gaining acceptance. When presentation brings in-

difference or rejection, it is wiser for staff to be self critical rather than to pour out venom upon their superiors.

With the need for persuasion recognized, thorough preparation is the obvious next step. Proposals which are half baked, couched in the wrong language, full of unanswered questions, lacking in objectivity, or semantically offensive, are doomed from the start, even when these fatal flaws affect only some minor part of the whole. To avoid all of them all of the time is impossible; to avoid most of them most of the time takes great artistry, but at least one can be conscious of the need.

Even with these conditions satisfied, defeat is quite possible, unless the staff man is adaptable. This connotes much more than fast footwork and a placating manner in a conference. Too often, those who would persuade others are over-identified with their own ideas and fearful that acceptance of suggested modifications will cost them credit for the conception of which they are so proud. This leads in turn to insistence upon adoption unchanged or no adoption at all—and results inevitably in no adoption.

In fact, rigid pride of authorship is the best means of *not* persuading people that I know, because it ignores a basic facet of human behavior. The staff man who will not have his ideas changed by jot or tittle acts as he does because they are *his* ideas; he is identified with them. Ergo, if he wants to motivate his superior to accept them and act upon them, the best way to do so is to get the superior identified too, and there is no better way to do this than to accept the superior's suggestions. Doing so will convert him from a possible opponent to a participant and proponent.

This in no sense advocates that the staff man behave like a sycophant. If the critic's suggestion is sound, by all means be adaptable and accept the proposed change. If the proposed change is unsound, do not accept it merely because it comes from a superior; reject it but in doing so give evidence of objectivity and responsiveness. These terms are just as much a part of adaptability as acceptance itself.

Patience, that sterling virtue, is requisite to persuasion too. On more than one occasion I have had my own staff proposals rejected and then, strangely, have seen acceptance follow at a later time. As far as I could see nothing had happened but the passage of time and, perhaps, chance for assimilation. From these experiences I have come to fancy that time is a separate and independent ally in the art of persuasion.

Finally, as in so many administrative matters, the ethical content of persuasion must be mentioned. To have one's ideas accepted and adopted the need for persuasion must be perceived and acted upon by thorough preparation, adaptability, and patience. These stratagems are important but much less so than the reputation of the persuader. Succeed in persuading at the cost of objectivity, or for self service, or by sycophancy, and the chance of persuading next time is lessened. Witness the boy who cried wolf. Succeed with objectivity, with subordination of self, and with candor, and each successive proposal wins favor more easily. To the staff man, as to all others as well, virtue is more than just its own reward.

6

In these pages I have attempted an examination of the staff relationship that is important to almost every present day organization.

Toward superiors and peers staff behaves reasonably well in accordance with the convention of giving advice within the area of expert knowledge. Toward line subordinates staff does not observe the advisory convention, because of presumed expertness and higher rank. The tendency of staff to become functional over line subordinates has been decried as destructive of line decisiveness and detrimental to the attainment of proper staff goals. Prevention of these tendencies may come about from subordinate resistance or from direction by superiors but is most likely to result from staff perception and self discipline.

The natural advisory relationship toward superiors and peers raises questions of persuasiveness and the assignment of staff purpose. A strong argument has been made for the specific encouragement of staff imagination and creativeness beyond the mere rendering of sought for advice.

Lacking authority, staff must be aware of the strategy and tactics of persuasion, of the need for thorough preparation, adaptability and participation, and the ingredient of patience. Above all, the need for objectivity and continued ethical behavior has been given as prerequisite to satisfactory staff achievement.

VIII

On Operations Analysis

AMONG the staff elements of organization which have multiplied in recent years are those engaged in the analysis of operations. Their tasks are described variously: as operations research, industrial engineering, operations analysis, operations evaluation, etc., terms which are not quite synonymous nor altogether acceptable to jealous practitioners in one or another of these fields. Here, however, they will mean the same thing: staff engaged in the analysis of operations with the mission of improving performance. Their goal is research rather than service.

Such elements of organization are presently active throughout industry, in the Army, Navy, and Air Force, and are spreading rapidly into government, business, finance, and transportation, and into the operations of hospitals and other eleemosynary organizations. My own opinion is that this almost explosive growth in operations analysis is a logical extension of the industrial revolution, potentially as far reaching in its effects as the spinning jenny or the steam engine. Separate discussion could be justified for this reason but that is not the purpose here. Operations analysis, as one of many staff elements, differs administratively from all of the others.

2

Operations analysis differs from other staff because it must perform its tasks under handicaps not imposed upon any other comparable organization group.

First among these handicaps is the implication, natural to the environment of operations analysis, that the analyst is not an expert, but on the contrary quite inexpert, in the very operation that he is subjecting to scrutiny. He, the analyst, cannot perform the operation himself, possibly he has never before seen it performed. Those who can perform it have done so for a long time with fluency and skill. How can it be presumed that a stranger can tell experienced and expert operators how to do their job better?

The idea is preposterously contrary to our own notions about ourselves. All of us perform "operations" of one sort or another in the ordinary routines of living; the idea that some observer can tell us how to do better is naturally repugnant, and repugnance creates conflict between those being analyzed and the operations analyst. Other staff may face this obstacle, but only rarely. Usually the statistician deals with statistics, the meteorologist with weather, the lawyer with legal matters, the financier with money, and each is accepted as more expert in his own field than those in the line organization. The operations analyst deals with operations and is tacitly assumed to be less expert than the line people who perform them. This attitude is implicit in the operations analysis relationship.

Whether hostility from line organization people is open or covert, weak or strong, will depend upon several things. If the operation under study involves no human elements, there will be no hostility, of course, and in these somewhat rare cases the operations analyst can be as peaceful as any other staff dealing with inanimate, unemotional objects. The potential for hostility, one might say, depends upon the human relations content of the operation to be analyzed. If there are people whose performance is to be studied, they are likely to look upon the operations analyst and the possibility of operational improvements from his work with a very jaundiced eye.

The degree of hostility also will depend upon the previous history of operations analysis in the organization, and the current health of the enterprise. If operations analysis has previously demonstrated that investigators of this kind *can* show improvements to experienced performers, then current projects have a better chance for favorable reception. If the organization is in desperate straits, in a "root-hog-or-die" condition, then the analyst also may be received well, on the chance that he may be the doctor who can save the dying patient. And the converse may also be true; the very healthy organization may receive the operations analyst with favor or with an open mind, because in these situations the line personnel to be studied may feel secure enough to be complacent.

3

Hostility to operations analysis derives from yet another, closely related source: an imputation of criticism of operating personnel.

In almost every enterprise there are many operations and operations analysis must select from among them. Such a choice implies something wrong in the way the chosen operation is now being performed and this in turn suggests something wrong with those performing the task. Such imputations can be mitigated by preliminary diplomacy but cannot be erased altogether.

The product of such inferences is a sense of insecurity and its result is, as before, hostility. Those in operations feel criticised and invariably wonder what will happen to them as the security of the status quo is threatened. Although the ugly word never may be spoken, the analyst may be suspected as a spy, who will perceive what operating personnel are doing and report back to the boss their individual and group shortcomings. Then, as a direct consequence of operations analysis, the axe will fall.

Such a fear would be natural even in a virgin situation but, unfortunately, operations analysis can have no virgin situations; it has a history and that history supports the fear. From the time that Frederick W. Taylor first studied Schmidt loading pig iron and then the yard shovellers at Bethlehem, the consequences of operations analysis have all too frequently been punitive. Operating personnel have been displaced in veritable droves, their conduct has been shaped according to the notions of an "inexpert" outsider, their tempi of work have been uncomfortably and sometimes ruthlessly speeded. Historically, operations analysis has danced and now must pay the piper.

These familiar points are not made to cast reflection upon Taylor's great achievements or to castigate the operations analysts of bygone decades. Theirs was a different society and they behaved in accordance with its mores, just as we would have done and now do. The point relates only to the pursuit of operations analysis today, a staff role that is made uniquely difficult by the natural presumption of inexpertness, by the implication of criticism of operating personnel, by the creation of insecurity and fear of the analyst as a spy, and, finally, by a history that suggests unpleasant consequences to the subjects of today's investigations.

4

These forces impose severe requirements upon operations analysts and upon administrators to whom such investigators report. All that has been said previously about persuasiveness as a requirement of staff success must now be compounded, for the operations analyst must be diplomatic, persuasive, self-effacing, objective, adaptive, and patient, before, during, and after his investigations. If he is not, if he is oblivious of the inherent forces of hostility, or unsuccessful in mitigating them, his chances of sound research or fruitful result are seriously impaired or blocked entirely. Mild or overt opposition to operations analysis can all too easily modify behavior and yield misleading or meaningless information and conclusions. And, even when good data are obtainable, the opposition of operating personnel can, quite literally, sabotage results. In operations analysis there is no substitute for that valuable and elusive quality: cooperation.

Operations analysts often fall short of perfection in the exercise of this art, as might be expected. They do so because they are frail human beings but also because they become excessively preoccupied with the numbers generated by their studies. Engaged as they so often are in providing quantitative information for decision making by line executives, they forget that their mathematical models, time standards, and incentive formulas will represent organization behavior only with the consent of operating personnel, from executives to rank and file. Much more will be said about administrative reverence for numbers; it suffices now to emphasize that successful operations analysis, at the present state of the art, depends as much upon human as upon technical skills.

5

Even when its practitioners are technically competent and perceptive and skillful in human relations, operations analysis cannot succeed in the face of apathy or misdirected support from line administration. Nor can operations analysis succeed for the executive who is looking for precise qualification, for "push button" decision making. The degree of perception and understanding required of line administrators is even greater than has been depicted thus far.

Administrators of operations analysis cannot alter, undo, or make over the history that has been described as a handicap. But history always is in the making and it is they, the line administrators, who shape that history in their own enterprises by using operations analysis.

An example will illustrate the point. An industrial engineering team making a study of the composition of newspaper advertising quickly perceived that many advertisers correct their proofs so extensively that the original typesetting, proofreading, and correcting must be thrown away or reset. It was easy to point out, when the behavior of advertisers could be predicted, that proofreading and correcting in the newspaper composing room should be eliminated.

The operations analysis group was perceptive enough to see that adoption of this proposal would, by a small but significant amount, reduce available employment to some proofreaders and compositors, in an industry whose labor force, having experienced the introduction of the linotype, the stereotype, and the teletype, is extremely sensitive to the loss of "situations."

One of the publishers, an astute and progressive one, to

whom these observations were made during field studies, adopted the change forthwith—and met with prompt opposition from the local union. Settlement of the mild dispute was agreeable enough and a saving was realized but this point can be made: the next attempt at operations analysis in that composing room—and perhaps in others too—will have a harder time because of that decision. Operations analysis costs jobs; therefore it should be opposed by workers.

The only alternative to this kind of precipitate action is protection of the potentially displaced workers, by other jobs, by some form of compensation, or until attrition has reduced the force to the level required by the easier method. All of these cost money, postpone realization of the saving and, seemingly, reduce the net gain.

Seemingly, but not really. Operations analysis has value, value that is diminished by some indefinable amount by the kind of punitive action that has been described. If that value is greater than the cost of deferring labor displacement, then a decision to defer obviously is the proper one, not because it is humane, considerate, or compassionate, but because it will yield the greatest net profit. The administrator can be as hardheaded and cold blooded as he pleases; all that is asked here is consideration of *all* of the ingredients affecting the decision.

There is another, mandatory way of saying this: for maximum continuing return, operations analysis invariably must be accompanied by analysis of the optimum means of adopting the proposals made.

6

This requirement of perceptive, active support by line administration must be buttressed by mutual understanding of another facet of operations analysis. It is not enough for those engaged in such work to submit recommendations to line executives, win approval and a favorable decision, and then retire from the fray, to study new problems and make new recommendations. If this is the course of events, the proposed operational changes will die aborning.

Responsibility for overcoming the obstacles of introduction and transition belongs to the operations analysts who conceived, created, and espoused the proposed change. During the introductory stage of a new development, staff must become at least to some degree operational and must remain in that relationship until the new method has been successfully launched. Only then should the operations analysts withdraw for engagement in new projects.

This need is strongly emphasized, because many operations analysts have been frustrated and many administrators disappointed when sound studies and good recommendations have passed into limbo despite executive approval. It is a cold fact that conception, recommendation, and approval do not get a new method to the halfway mark. The hump of the road requires the push of those who care about the new way through identification with it, that is to say, the operations analysts. They should specifically be assigned to the task of introduction. When transition has been completed, they should, with equal specificity, be assigned to new projects in analysis, lest they settle into operations in the manner previously described.

These paragraphs have been pretty strong and some may wonder why. The answer, I think, is fairly simple: operations analysis, beyond all other staff agencies, presents proposals which call for changes, often dramatic, in human behavior. These cannot be had by executive order.

Many executives know this intuitively but shrink from the time and investment required for effective transition.

This explains, I suspect, the great preoccupation with new machines and "hardware" exhibited by so many industrial executives. The speed of the assembly line may be increased by use of new tools but not by new methods alone; a machine running well below capacity cannot be speeded simply by resetting the rheostat, but the same transition can be effected by replacement with a new and faster machine. New machines, new tools, new gadgetry are called "technological change," and this is semantically virtuous. New methods which can have the same result are a "speed up," and this is semantically evil.

This is chiefly a description of current industrial mores but the illustration serves further to emphasize the requirement that operations analysts see their proposals through the introductory stage.

7

Finally, at some risk of redundancy, mention must be made again of persuasiveness, with special reference to operations analysis.

The best way to win acceptance of research into operations and to get proposed changes adopted is to enlist the participation of operating personnel in each investigation. This is an obvious technique, to be sure; enlisting participation will identify the operators with the venture, the proposed changes then will be "theirs," and so become acceptable to them. Q.E.D.

However, the statement is not nearly so obvious as it sounds. If participation is enlisted as a "technique," in the sense that it is employed to manipulate people, it may work for a time but not for long. The word "Machiavellian" has not endured nor kept its connotations because the Prince was noted for his sincerity or candor.

No. Continued success in operations analysis requires a

genuine sharing of the discoveries, the hazards, the fruits, and the glory, between those in operations and those in operations analysis.

8

Operations analysis has been described as an activity presenting problems to administration which are different from those created by other staff. Until a reputation has been earned, the operations analyst will be regarded as less expert than those he studies and resented as a critic and possible spy.

These inherent forces of hostility have been augmented by the history of operations analysis, a history made by those who have not understood the economy of what so aptly has been called "enlightened selfishness." The individual administrator can do much to circumvent these obstacles by insisting that his operations analyst subordinates not only propose the changes to be made but also the means by which change is to be effected. To this end their assignments must carry through the introductory stages of their projects, or there will be no fulfillment of them.

Throughout these pages, repeated inferences have stressed the value and importance of objectivity, diplomacy, adaptability, patience, consideration, compassion, understanding, sincerity, candor, and selflessness. Repeated emphasis upon virtue and rectitude certainly is preaching and would be out of place here but for one fact: the operations analyst and his organization superior seek to change the ways of people. To that end these attributes are as essential and as economically valuable as scientific knowledge and technical skill.

IX

On the Deification of Numbers

URING the spring of 1942 an organization change brought about by World War II gave me a new boss or, more exactly, an old boss who returned to active administration to replace a younger man who had left to join the War Production Board in Washington.

Not long after this change occurred a front office conference was called to discuss the general subject of work ahead of the plant during the ensuing six months. It was agreed that some quantitative expression of available unsold capacity would be highly desirable, even essential, to the establishment of sound sales policy in the then seller's market. As staff engineer it fell to my lot to develop these numbers.

I was told at the outset that this was an easy mission, that the production superintendent kept an "allotment book" which showed present and future commitments in terms of man and machine hours. All that was necessary was scrutiny of the allotment book, computation of total available hours, and subtraction of committed hours. The remainder would be hours available for sale within the designated period.

Examination of the allotment book was more than a little disappointing; it showed, as future commitments, work that had been completed and it failed to show commitments for the future that had been made. Moreover, the graphic portrayal (by squares on ruled paper) of plant ca-

pacity obviously bore little relation to machine or man
hours. In short, there did not exist any mechanism for measurement to provide the numbers wanted.

I reported this to my boss and was told, never mind, there
wasn't time to set up a system of measurement, he *had* to
have these data to run the business, I should do the necessary additions and subtractions from the allotment book as
it was, he'd take care that the resulting figures were used
with discretion. Use the allotment book was in effect my
instruction.

I can no longer remember the results of this calculation
but it will do to say that 1000 machine hours were shown
to be available for sale during the remainder of the year.
With this figure I returned to the boss's office, was asked
for the result, and again demurred, saying that I was re-
luctant to give the number on the ground that it was just as
apt to mislead as to lead. I probably repeated my conviction
that the numbers were no good, as a part of my demurrer.
The result, in any case, was somewhat explosive and not a
little peremptory; I was denounced as bull-headed and told
to hand over the data forthwith. He'd be the judge of its
validity.

A few days later there was a sales conference to which I
was invited. The boss began the meeting by this simple
statement, "We have 1000 hours unsold between now and
January 1." Once more I couldn't resist and responded,
sotto voce from the back of the room, "I'll be damned if we
do." This more or less broke up the meeting. The boss exploded and did not recover his equanimity until later, when
he coldly informed me that, if I was so smart, I could have
the job of developing a system for measuring capacity and
commitments and that I had better do so pretty quickly.

Perhaps the reader can in some way discern between these

lines the affection that existed between this man and me, and perhaps also the humor that threaded through these sessions, explosive as some of them were. The anecdote is not told on this account but to illustrate the beguiling power of numbers, not just in this one plant at this one time over this one exceedingly capable executive, but in the whole domain of administration. Numbers always tend to dominate administrative decisions, even when such numbers as are available are grossly inaccurate or inadequate.

2

Chester Barnard in his very perceptive paper, "Mind in Everyday Affairs"[1] has said that three kinds of considerations govern decision making: material that consists of precise information, material of hybrid character, and material of a speculative type. The first of these he describes as those elements of a decision which may be expressed in numbers, the second "data of poor quality or limited extent," and the third "impressions and probabilities not susceptible of mathematical expression and purely contingent uncertainties."

I can add only one thing to Mr. Barnard's analysis and that is the observation already made: numbers tend inordinately to dominate decision making. They do this in two ways: first, by crowding out or pushing aside those intangibles which cannot be quantified but which may exceed in importance that which is measurable and, second, by acquiring an aura of accuracy which leads the decision maker to forget that numbers sometimes have dubious validity. Both of these tendencies suppress or subordinate judgment

[1] Appended to Mr. Barnard's *Functions of the Executive*. Cambridge, Harvard University Press, 1947.

and accord to numbers a dogmatic and sacred quality which I have characterized as the deification of numbers.

This is not to be taken as an argument against numbers in decision making. Not at all. As my boss inferred, one has to have numbers to run a business; the more numbers there are and the more accurate they are the better.

This point can be emphasized by contrasting an optimum role of numbers in decision making with the role that numbers too often play. Ideally, one might say, decisions should be made by: (1) maximizing the available quantitative information; (2) according to the quantitative elements only that degree of confidence merited by the numbers; (3) giving due and proper weight to all other intangible, nonquantifiable factors.

What usually happens is something more nearly like this: decisions are made by: (1) maximizing the available precise information; (2) according to *all* of the numbers complete and total confidence; (3) allowing the numbers to set aside, negate, and dominate the intangible elements, even when these are of overriding importance. Steps, or rather *missteps* (2) and (3) are the targets of these arguments, not the collection and use of numbers per se.

3

For initial exemplification I need not go outside my own field of industrial engineering. Industrial engineers often are engaged in supplying numbers to line management, usually in the form of time standards. By measuring with a stop watch the performance of one or more workers on a given task the industrial engineer is able to say that the standard time for that task is x minutes per piece, or y hours per pound, or z minutes per 100, or whatever relationship is suitable for the operation at hand. Management can then use these numbers in scheduling, in cost accounting, in estimating for price setting, and in the compensation of workers through some incentive plan.

An industrial enterprise cannot be run successfully without using numbers for all of these things. Schedules must be made, hour costs known, prices quoted, and workers paid. Sometimes in very small outfits deliveries are promised and prices quoted by hunch, without the use of arithmetic but, even so, one cannot do any of these four things without using a number. So far, there are only two known ways of obtaining such numbers for managerial use: experience, or the use of time study. Of these, time study is by far the better way.

But—and this is the essence of the matter here—time study, with all its superiority over the acquisition of data by experience, is still a process which yields inexact information to management, that is to say, time standards themselves have tolerances about "true" values. Their ranges of inaccuracy are much, much less than from data derived from experience but, even so, the tolerance limits of the superior technique are still too large to be ignored by administrators.

While the purpose here is not to explore time study, a few reasons for the inexactness of the process are in order. To measure performance and set a time standard the industrial engineer must measure one or more workers, at one or more times, under one or more sets of operating conditions. Obviously, measurements taken of Worker A from 9 to 10 A.M. may reflect differences in materials, tools, instructions, fatigue, motivation, and aptitude from measurements taken of Worker B from 3 to 4 P.M. on another day. To narrow the errors caused by these sources of variation the industrial engineer traditionally has said that his standards are intended to enable the "average worker working with average effort under average conditions" to attain the standard.

When the stop-watch study is made, the observer seeks to relate the tempo of the worker before him to a mind's-eye image of the average worker and to "rate" his subject accordingly. Thus he may say that a fast, apt, and diligent worker is rated at 125 per cent of normal and a slow, inept, and slothful worker at 75, 80, or some other per cent of normal. The shorter stop watch readings on the first man will be multiplied by 1.25 and the slower readings on the second by 0.75, and the general idea is that the two products will be equal, if the readings and ratings have been made correctly.

To compensate for the cumulative effects of fatigue over the working day the stop watch data are also multiplied by a "fatigue allowance" or "fatigue factor," empirically set in the range of 10 or 20 per cent. Thus, the emergent time standard S, is the product of stop watch readings W, an empirical fatigue allowance F, and a subjectively chosen rating factor R:

$$S = W \times F \times R.$$

The result, obviously, must be inexact; it can't be anything else. Industrial engineers laudably are doing a great deal to diminish the range of time standards' inaccuracies and are themselves—that is, the good ones—the foremost critics of time study's weaknesses but the fact remains that there are millions of time standards in use throughout industry and they are all, for administrative purposes, inexact numbers.

Many wise administrators realize and remember this but the vast majority do not. These, in sub-conscious yearning—that's exactly what it is—for quantification to relieve them of the uncertainties of judgment in decision making, look upon the time standards, set by use of a stop watch and expressed in three or four significant figures, as accurate. If a worker doesn't come up to standard, it is *his* fault; if a department doesn't show standard efficiency, the foreman is advised to get on the ball; if the union protests that a standard is "tight," the complaint is denounced as an attempt to stir up trouble. The standard must not be questioned. It is "right," an assertion often made to the accompaniment of table thumping.

In the last chapter I said that the mathematical models achieved by operations analysts represent organization behavior only with the consent of line personnel, from executives to rank and file. Time standards, as numbers which establish performance goals, are mathematical models intended to represent organization behavior. They do so only with the consent[2] of the operators and supervisors who work under them. A time standard is "right" only when these people *think* it is. For numbers such as these, psychological "rightness" is of much greater significance and value than arithmetic.

In most organizations, as I have said, little or no attention is paid to psychological factors and the inexact numbers of time study are converted in the minds of administrators from quasi-precise to precise. The results of this conversion are administrative delusion, employee, union and supervisory hostility, and evasive reporting of performance. The numbers furnished by time study are much more accurate than those derived from experience; they diminish the elements

[2] For the word *consent* in this connection I am indebted to William Gomberg: "Above all, in a democratic society he (the industrial engineer) must understand the relationship between efficiency and consent." Quoted from "Trade Unions and Industrial Engineering," *Handbook of Industrial Engineering and Management*. Englewood Cliffs, N. J., Prentice-Hall, 1955.

requiring administrative judgment but they do not eliminate judgment. The mistake is to assume that they do.

4

The use of numbers by industrial executives to make decisions pro or con about new equipment is analogous to, yet curiously different from, the foregoing time study example.

Proposals for replacing existing equipment or a present manufacturing method by new equipment or a better method usually are considered by comparing the total annual cost by the present method with the prospective annual cost by the new way. Labor, maintenance, power, tools, rent, interest, depreciation, installation, training, raw material consumption, spoilage, all may be considered in great detail, with the expectation, of course, that the new way will show to advantage. The difference between the new way and the old is the prospective annual saving, if the new method is adopted and the new machine purchased.

This prospective annual saving then is divided into the investment required for the new equipment, machine, or method, and the quotient is spoken of as the number of years required for the investment to "pay for itself." In many, indeed most, cases, decisions favorable to new investment will be made only if the "pay-out time" is three years or less. Three is not always the choice but, whatever the choice, this is the number that is deified.

The reasoning involved, if one may call it that, is curious and vulnerable. At the very time that the executive is demanding, as a condition pre-requisite to investment, a very short payout period, he is apt to be predicating a long remaining life for present equipment and even greater longevity for that which is proposed. The proper question, therefore, is not whether enough will be saved in three years or less but whether probable profit will be attractively augmented over the estimated life span of the market of the product being made or the equipment being used. This, more reasonable point of view often is lost in blind obedience to a number and a rule: if the pay-out time is n years or less, buy; if it is more than n years, don't. Decisions of very great importance are made in just this way.

This is not intended as a criticism of conservative investment policy, for there are very good reasons for caution in making investment decisions: the desirability of preserving liquid capital, uncertainties in the market place, uncertainties in obsolescence and depreciation, the chance of sub-par performance by a new machine, the costly turbulence that a new technology always creates within an organization. These are reasons enough for caution. My quarrel is not with investment conservatism, not at all, but only with *blind* conservatism. Evaluation and decision should depend upon consideration of present and prospective costs *and* conscious consideration of the uncertainties as well. Too frequently costs alone are considered; the uncertainties are vaguely in the background and the executive knee is bent in obeisance to a number.

5

Yet another example can be drawn from research on military operations. Scientists working in this field, by means of ingenious techniques called "operation gaming" and "Monte Carlo methods," have learned to "fight" small scale "battles" on electronic computers. By doing so they can learn something about the relative worth of different weapons and can supply quantitative information to military commanders to assist them in weapons procurement.

As in the case of the industrial manager, the military commander cannot operate without numbers. He must decide to equip his force with X mortars, Y trucks, and Z tanks and, within these and other classifications of equipment, he must make quantitative choices. Shall he spend his available money (the amount itself is a limited quantity) on more tanks and fewer trucks, or vice versa? Shall he elect to buy light, medium, or heavy tanks, or some of each?

Military administrators can answer these questions only by judgment and experience, aided by cost and performance data. In peace time they can not fight real battles to test the value of each weapon and such trials and maneuvers as can be simulated are unsatisfactory, expensive, and generally inconclusive. In contrast to this the computer can fight 100 battles in an hour and by so doing tell the commander something about the relative virtues of, say, light versus medium tanks.

But to do this the computer must be given a set of rules by which the game or battle is to be played. Each class of tank must be assigned capabilities of movement and firepower, the probabilities of movement in a given direction must be formulated, and the rules must say under what sets of conditions one tank will "kill" the other, or vice versa. All of these rules must be expressed in numbers.

In the case of probable direction of movement this is done by a grid system whereby the individual tank in the center square (Fig. 3) may make any one of nine moves: it may stay where it is or move to any one of the eight surrounding squares. The direction of movement chosen by the tank commander will depend upon the whereabouts of the enemy and the characteristics of the terrain: height, cover, condition, etc. Thus a given tank will be much more likely to move in the direction of the enemy to high, firm ground with

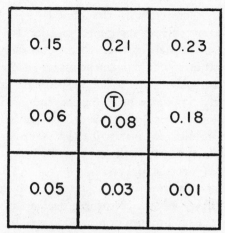

Fig. 3. Movement probabilities in a grid.

good cover than away from the enemy into an exposed marsh. [3]

The probabilities of each move are estimated as indicated in Fig. 3, where the likelihood of a move into the marsh in the south-east corner is given as 0.01 while that of a move to high ground toward the enemy is given as 0.23 for the square in the north-east corner. (The sum of the probabilities for each move is, of course, 1.0.) By programming the computer

[3] Richard E. Zimmerman, "A Monte Carlo Model for Military Analysis," *Operations Research for Management*, Vol. 2, pp. 382–383. Baltimore, The Johns Hopkins Press, 1956. ". . . *maneuver* is related to the average terrain characteristics of the 100-meter grid squares into which the battlefield is divided. . . . The features of these grid squares that are stored in the computer are: (1) elevation to nearest meter; (2) degree of concealment provided by vegetation on square in quarter-steps of from zero to full concealment; (3) existence of significant terrain features: swamp, crest of hill, steep hill; and (4) the speed with which a given combat unit can cross the square. These features are used to compute the relative probabilities that each of the neighboring squares should (or would!) be selected as the next position. Once the probabilities are available a Monte Carlo choice is made among the possible positions." The figures shown in the squares of Fig. 3 have been assumed by me for purposes of illustration and are not drawn from Zimmerman's work.

to agree with these probabilities, that is, 23 chances for a move to the north-east square to one for the south-east square, and by repeating the process for each successive move for each tank, the movement aspect of the game may be played. Similarly, other attributes of each kind of tank may be played simultaneously on the computer according to the established rules. A series of such games will yield quantitative results, e.g., in 50 battles X tanks of Type A are killed against $1\frac{1}{2}$ X tanks of Type B, a clear indication that Type A is superior to Type B.

The persuasive nature of these results is quite apparent. Now the military administrator can decide to buy Type A to the diminution or elimination of Type B, which got licked in 50 battles fought in one of those wonderful, mysterious, foolproof computers. It is easy, too easy, to forget that the results are not one bit better than the assumptions put into the computer in the first place. Should the rules neglect a performance attribute wherein B is superior to A, the results will mislead. Should estimates of relative fire-power be distorted, so will the answers. Should the probabilities of movement be estimated badly, the answers will be shifted one way or the other.

Clearly, then, these quantitative results are not precise. They have very great value to the administrator, as long as they are recognized for what they are: *additional* information to aid military commanders to make decisions about weapons. As such, they diminish but do not erase the uncertainties of administrative judgment.

6

The foregoing example does not describe administrative misuse of numbers in being and, it may be hoped, it will not describe administrative misuse of numbers in prospect. It does, however, describe the quest for numbers that is current in so many fields of management. Operation gaming, Monte Carlo methods, linear programming, queueing theory, time study, accounting, statistical quality control, aptitude testing, job evaluation, merit rating are all examples of the same thing: the quantification of attributes which are essential to decision making in every kind of organization.

Every one of these techniques is of very great value, not merely in supplying numbers, but also in compelling systematic and analytical consideration of all of the facets of an administrative problem.

The administrator who neglects these tools, who overly prides himself on judgment and runs his outfit "by the seat of his pants"—there are, unfortunately, some of these too—is infinitely worse off than the executive who searches for all the quantitative information he can get.

The industrial executive who does not use cost accounting is, to speak harshly, a fool, but his counterpart who uses it and forgets that it depicts the past and not the future is no paragon of administrative virtue either. (How often executives speak of "actual" costs in the present tense, as though they know such figures with precision. How often they forget that the distributions of overhead are matters of judgment.)

Similarly, the personnel manager who uses aptitude testing to select and place employees is wisely making use of available quantification, but his wisdom may be vitiated if he forgets that such tests do not correlate perfectly with achievement on the job, which is the true criterion. (I once heard an executive tell a subordinate that the tests showed he was dumb, and knew of another promising young man who was for a time "branded" by such tests as lacking in self-confidence, surely a trait that must change with accomplishment.)

Other examples are more subtle than these. Seniority clauses in labor contracts are not usually thought of as quantitative processes but that is exactly what they are, for they compel decisions on layoff, transfer, or promotion on the basis of the number of years, days, and months worked, to the neglect or exclusion of such qualitative factors as cooperation, diligence, productivity, attendance, punctuality, loyalty, and responsibility. And often the dominance of the number of days worked does violence to equity as well.

Teachers in public education are exposed to the same kind of thing. Earnings rise, not only with the passage of time and accumulation of experience, but also in rigidly prescribed ways for possession of the bachelor's degree, the master's degree, the doctor's degree, or for college credits between these achievement levels. We do not think of the possession or lack of a college degree as a quantitative matter but that is what it is, a one or nothing affair. No one disputes the value of these criteria; they are properly part of any decision to promote or not to promote. But does an A.B., an M.A., a Ph.D., or 200 college credits, or ten years of experience certify that the possessor thereof is a *teacher* deserving promotion? The question answers itself. Qualities of inspiration, eloquence, consideration, interest, devotion are very difficult to evaluate but that does not mean that these vital elements should be smothered, set aside, neglected, by the easier-to-get but less important numbers.

In the university to which I am attached students have been graduated with fewer than the usual number of courses and credits, if the quality of work has been high. Conversely, others have been denied graduation with more than the usual number of courses, if the quality of work has been low. Still others have been asked to leave by exercise of the same kind of faculty (i.e., executive) judgment. This, I think, is administratively sound and conducive to equity. An atmosphere of devotion to quality desirably pervades the institution.

But, even in this wholesome atmosphere, the deification of numbers is perceptible. Let a faculty member be brought forward for promotion and observe what happens. There are few rules but there is a customary procedure. An *ad hoc* committee is appointed to evaluate the proposed promotion; they gather biographical, bibliographical and reference information about the candidate and bring forth a statement of recommendation, deferral, or denial, all a very thoroughgoing and judicious process.

As discussion of the matter develops one perceives that the candidate's bibliography comes more and more to the fore. Philosophically there will be agreement on the importance of teaching ability, imagination, compatibility, interest in students, research ability, and the like but, practically, in the instant case, the bibliography tends to dominate. No one measures the typed list of publications with a ruler or counts the items, or weighs the stack of reprints, but nonetheless, this kind of mind's-eye quantification is going on, with the result that the inspiring teacher or ingenious experimenter who doesn't publish has a harder time in winning promotion than his more prolific colleague, who may be of less worth in the classroom or laboratory.

Thus, the beguiling and persuasive power of numbers sways even those organizations which are most sensitive to qualitative values. When this happens, when numbers are deified, they are detrimental to sound decisions. Maximize their availability, yes, but do not forget their sometimes inaccuracy, nor let them subjugate those elements of decision which cannot be quantified.

X

On Forecasting

THE terms *forecasting* and *planning*, often used synonymously in administration and management, here will be given different meanings. Forecasting, the subject of this chapter, will mean prediction, the act of anticipating in some formal and quantitative way a future goal, status, or attainment of an enterprise. Planning, the subject of the next chapter, will describe the act of separating the mental and manual portions of an operation, in order that the mental effort required may be transferred to some preliminary "planning" stage. Thus, planning will be considered as a kind of extension of the principle of division of labor, something altogether different from the attribute of prediction which will be accorded to forecasting.

2

To a greater or less extent everyone is compelled to engage in forecasting in the course of everyday living. We agree to be at a certain place at a certain time, we engage to attend a specified meeting to be held in the future, we pledge ourselves to complete tasks of various kinds, we make a variety of commitments, all of which require us to predict our future behavior and performance in some way.

Much of this kind of forecasting is taken for granted, of course. Sometimes we may pause to consider the certainty or uncertainty of fulfillment, or to assess the relative priority of other, possibly conflicting commitments, but often predictions of this kind will be made by all of us without much analysis or cerebration. And still more often, forecasts of this kind will be made without awareness that they are essentially quantitative predictions. To agree to be at a stated place at a stated time is a commitment which can be described precisely and uniquely in numbers: one man—his identity can be established by a number (e.g., his social security number)—is to be at the specified intersection of two coordinates of longitude and latitude at the specified day and hour. All of these are expressible in numbers.

While this is too fanciful to be taken seriously, there is a point to be made, namely, that forecasting is essentially a quantitative process and use of forecasting by administrators is a part of the general problem of administrative use of numbers.

3

With respect to the kind of forecasting that we all do routinely, one finds little administrative resistance to prediction. Nor does one find resistance to the forecasting of those things which are necessary to the individual organization. A merchant will quote the prices at which he is willing to sell his goods, a banker will stipulate the rate of interest he will pay on deposits, a jobbing manufacturer will specify a delivery date.

Administrators at various levels in these enterprises will give very careful attention to predictions of this kind, recognizing that price, rate of interest, and time for production are life and death matters to their respective organizations. The merchant will resist too low a price as ruinous, too high a price as non-competitive, and too long a price guarantee as risky, and the banker will be governed by similar restrictions. The jobbing manufacturer on his part will resist predicting a close delivery date if there is a penalty clause for being late, unless this risk is counterbalanced by a high price. There will be resistance, in short, to predictions which are deemed to be excessively risky but there will not be resistance to forecasts of this kind per se. They, and other predictions like them in other kinds of organizations, are accepted as necessary.

Beyond those forecasts which are routine and those which are compulsory, there are other areas in which administrators may, of their own volition, predict future states of their organizations for various reasons. The president of a university may forecast future student enrollment, not because he must, or because he expects to announce his predictions as commitments to the general public, but for purposes of administrative review and control. The merchant may forecast the geographical spread and rate of growth of his organization with the same administrative purposes in mind. The military commander may predict—indeed he *will* predict, because this comes close to necessity—the progress of his projected offensive, not because he expects to announce these goals to the enemy or to pledge them as commitments to his own people, but because this is the only way he can control and coordinate the many elements of the operation.

Toward this kind of forecasting, forecasting less attended by compulsion, more directed toward control and coordination, administrators behave—at least I have seen some of them behave—just as they do with respect to numbers generally: (1) they eschew forecasting on the ground that predictions cannot be made as precisely as railroad time tables; or (2) they forecast and thereupon deify the predictions, just as they deify other inexact numbers. Sometimes, of course, administrators exhibit one of these tendencies, sometimes the other, and, not infrequently, they resist, then deify in rapid sequence. Others, happily, forecast and use forecasting with wisdom and restraint.

4

To eschew forecasting, except when such action is compulsory, because of the inherent inaccuracy of predicting the future, is to ignore the review, coordinating, and control values of the process. These attributes, and the uncertainties of prediction as well, are illustrated in the Gantt Chart shown in Fig. 4.

This chart was made to portray the interrelationships and sequences involved in a plant expansion just after World War II. On other previous occasions this company had expanded by new construction, each time, however, without a forecast of the kind shown here. Since the enterprise is a relatively small one as industrial establishments go, a similar, informal procedure would have worked on this occasion too. Construction could have been arranged, machinery ordered, personnel hired and trained, and sales commitments on new capacity made as each event was ready for the next, or as executives were capable of anticipating readiness as each appropriate time drew near.

Quite possibly, this approach could have gone reasonably well. Machinery might have arrived on the scene just when construction had advanced far enough to permit erection. Personnel might have been hired just enough earlier for completion of sound training to coincide with completion of erection. And the sales department might have made just the right advance commitments to use the new people on the new machines in the new building at just the moment of readiness.

A series of such desirable coincidences under such circumstances is, of course, unlikely. More probably, machinery

ADDITIONS TO EQUIPMENT AND PERSONNEL

DEPARTMENT	PRESENT PERSONNEL	PROPOSED PERSONNEL	NOV.	DEC.	JAN.	FEB.	MARCH	APRIL	MAY	JUNE	JULY
PLANNING											
3T Dept.	3	4						HIRE ONE		TRAIN	
G3 Dept.	4	5		HIRE ONE		PRELIMINARY TRAINING	PRELIMINARY TRAINING	PRELIMINARY TRAINING		FINAL TRAINING	
G2-G20 Dept.	3	4						HIRE ONE		TRAIN	
A2 Dept.	3	4			HIRE ONE	PRELIMINARY TRAINING	PRELIMINARY TRAINING	PRELIMINARY TRAINING		FINAL TRAINING	
Accessories			PLAN NEED	ORDER	MANUFACTURE	MANUFACTURE					
KEYBOARD											
Machines	18	21		ORDER 2 / ORDER 1		MANUFACTURE	MANUFACTURE	INSTALL 2			INSTALL 1
Operators	27	36			HIRE FOUR		PRELIMINARY TRAINING	HIRE FIVE / PRELIMINARY TRAINING	PRELIMINARY TRAINING	FINAL TRAINING / PRELIMINARY TRAINING	
CASTERS											
Layout				LAYOUT	PLAN CONSTRUCTION		CONSTRUCT				
Machines	11	15		ORDER 2 / ORDER 2		MANUFACTURE	INSTALL 2 / MANUFACTURE				INSTALL 2
Operators	19	25			HIRE THREE		HIRE THREE / PRELIMINARY TRAINING	PRELIMINARY TRAINING	PRELIMINARY TRAINING	FINAL TRAINING / PRELIMINARY TRAINING	
PROOF ROOM											
Readers	7	9		HIRE ONE		TRAINING	HIRE ONE		TRAINING		
Copyholders	7	9		HIRE ONE	TRAINING		HIRE ONE	TRAINING			
Revisers	9	12		HIRE TWO		TRAINING	HIRE ONE		TRAINING		

Fig. 4. Portion of a Gantt Chart used in forecasting

would arrive too soon or too late for the moment of possible erection, personnel would be hired only after machinery was installed, and sales made only when the capacity to produce orders was actually available.

Even more likely—and this is part of the main point—delays would arise and be extended by "want of a nail—want of a shoe—want of a horse" phenomena. Machinery needs relative to construction would be anticipated and provided for because these are major items, large in the eyes of the executives concerned. But auxiliary equipment, small tools, etc., the "nails" and "shoes," without which the expansion cannot function, are apt to be forgotten in the absence of more systematic forecasting.

Following such a procedure of providing for needs as they are encountered or approached does ultimately result in a functioning enterprise, but only at a cost in delays and frictions which are certainly detrimental and perhaps even ruinous in a competitive environment. More formally and systematically predicting the multiple stages of the expansion can greatly reduce these delays and frictions but cannot, under even the best of circumstances, eliminate them. Thus it is a mistake to eschew forecasting because precise predictions are not possible, and it is equally a mistake to assume that forecasting, once done, yields perfect answers. Like so many other things in administration, forecasting yields better results only in a relative sense. The relative gain, however, is substantial.

5

For preparation of the chart itself there is required first of all a listing of all of the items relevant to the proposed expansion. The designer of the chart lists all of the things *he* can think of and the list is then exposed to the various executives concerned. They in turn fill in whatever may be missing, or modify what may be misstated, with the result that the chance of overlooking essential elements is greatly reduced. And, once an element has been listed, it cannot be forgotten.

Correspondingly, the designer's time predictions and interrelationships are exposed to group scrutiny and criticism. Like all numbers supplied to management, these should be made as precise as possible but it is obvious that some of the predicted intervals must be rough estimates and some must be based upon the predictions of those outside the organization, the contractor for construction and the machinery manufacturer—and their ability to predict and commit is limited in turn by just the same considerations. Upon this somewhat shaky foundation the internal predictions must be made: dates for hiring, durations of training, commitments for sales, all involving judgment of when to begin and how long to allow.

This is a critical stage of the forecast. Initial proposals by the designer will, as has been said, be exposed to group criticism and here each executive responsible for some portion of the program will be motivated, perhaps imperceptibly but no less really, by a desire to give himself as much time as possible. He will do this because he will know intuitively that the chart, once agreed upon, is apt to crystallize, ossify, petrify into a rigid mandate upon him. Choosing the numbers in the first place will be recognized as inexact; once chosen, their subjective origin is likely to be forgotten and each contributor will be expected to do or die to attain the stated goals.

Unless administration is conscious of this not too subtle force, the emergent forecast is apt to contain a good deal of needless cushion. The executive may squeeze some of this out by fiat, to be sure, but only at a heavy cost in loss of cooperation. It is much, much better to seek realistic agreement by emphasizing that the forecast goals will be used for what they are—inexact numbers—and not as cruel goads upon individual contributors to the program. A light spur, yes, a harsh goad, no.

Recognizing that inexact numbers in forecasting tend to become mandates and that this in turn leads to inflated estimates, a perceptive colleague has proposed introduction of the tolerance concept into forecasting procedures, using the Gantt Chart as a specific case (Fig. 5)[1]. While his proposal is sound from the standpoint of probability theory, my own opinion is that this is secondary to the psychological value of the idea. Introduction of a permissible tolerance range into a Gantt Chart, a budget, or any other kind of forecast can do these things: (1) keep before all concerned tangible evidence that the predictions are not precise, thereby reducing executive tendencies to deify the numbers; (2) mitigate and perhaps eliminate corollary tendencies to seek protective cushions; (3) thereby preserve cooperative attitudes toward the forecast as a whole. This idea deserves widespread adoption.

6

To get this far with a forecast, that is, to bring actually into being a set of predictions for administrative purposes, requires administrative consciousness of the need, willingness to forecast despite an absence of railroad accuracy, cognizance of the natural forces of inflation, and remembrance of the inexactness of the numbers used. With these

[1] Charles D. Flagle, Probability Based Tolerances in Forecasting and Planning. Informal Seminar in Operations Research. The Johns Hopkins University, Baltimore, 1954.

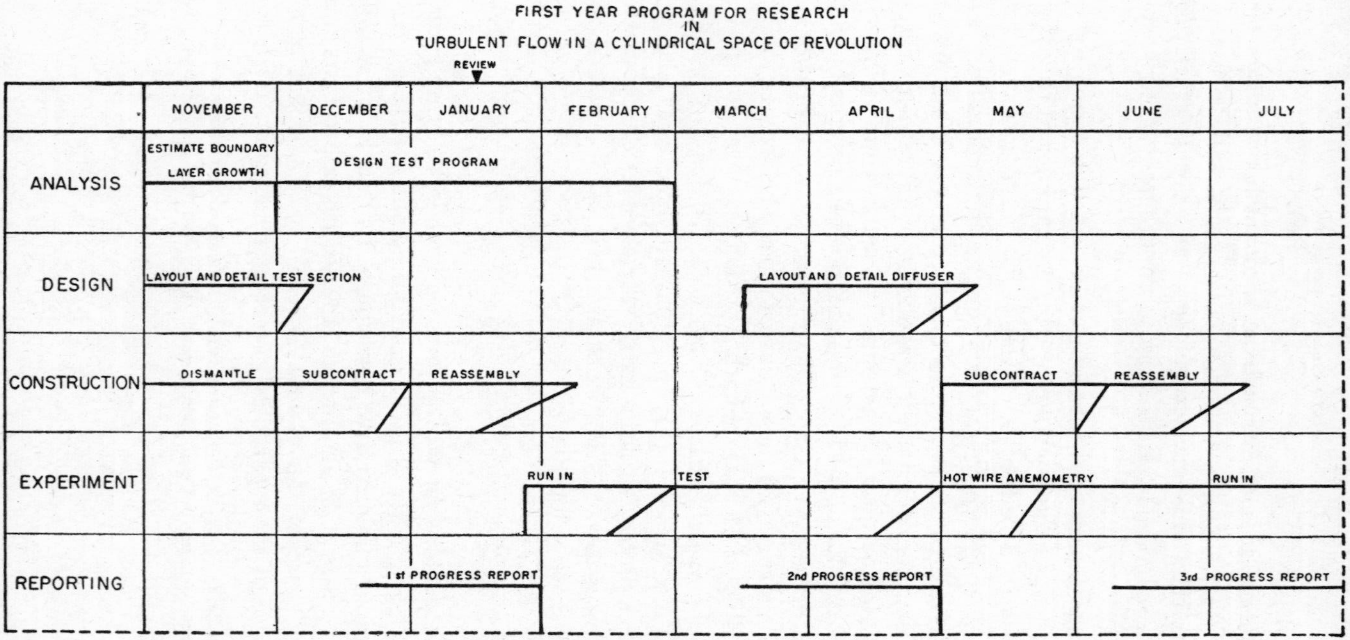

FIRST YEAR PROGRAM FOR RESEARCH
IN
TURBULENT FLOW IN A CYLINDRICAL SPACE OF REVOLUTION

Fig. 5. Introduction of tolerances in forecasting.

attributes in mind, the control and coordinating values of the forecast may be examined.

On the Gantt Chart (Fig. 4) each V along the top represents a date of group review. Each item at the left is considered individually; when the schedule has been met or bettered, a heavy line is drawn to close the lighter brackets; if the item is lagging behind the forecast, the heavy line is omitted altogether or drawn to a length proportional to the percentage of accomplishment. (These are conventional Gantt Chart techniques.)

Much more important is the consideration and formulation of appropriate administrative action, whenever the item is sufficiently out of hand to threaten disruption of the program. Various courses of action are available, of course, ranging from simple application of the aforesaid spur, through enhancing the resources allocated to the item, to extending the schedule or, for that matter, redrawing the chart to fit attainable predictions. Again, recollection that the predicted numbers are not exact is desirable for maintaining the best review atmosphere.

To this item by item evaluation is added review of the interrelationships portrayed by the chart. If machine procurement is lagging and cannot be bettered, there is no point in hiring, training, and paying workers to stand about and wait, nor any merit in committing sales that cannot be produced. The forecast clearly reveals these interdependencies and almost, one might say, forbids the administrator to forget or ignore them.

In the case illustrated these values were realized in practical ways. An initial chart had to be redrawn after the first review revealed its impracticability, chiefly because of an over-optimistic prediction on completion of construction, if memory serves correctly. A redrawn version was threatened in the same way by a machinery supplier who, on routine review inquiry, asked for much more time. This manufacturer was shown the chart and all that depended upon fulfillment of his original schedule. He was so impressed that he withdrew his demand for more time and made delivery as agreed. This is hardly typical but is illustrative. Similar, less dramatic results were achieved in other ways as well.

7

Forecasting, which has been defined as the act of predicting in quantitative terms for some administrative purpose, may be strategic in character, as in the case described, or may be tactical, as in routine scheduling or detailed budgeting. In all cases the numbers used should be given maximum attainable accuracy, but the inability to be precise should not lead the administrator to eschew forecasting. The values of formal prediction for coordination and control extend far beyond those forecasts which are conventional or compulsory, into the whole domain of administration.

When forecasts cannot be made with exactitude, it is wise to consider and adopt allowable tolerances, as means of preventing protective cushions, of insuring continued recognition of inexactness, and of preserving cooperation among those contributing to the goals set forth. The numbers used in forecasting, like all others used by administrators, do not deserve deification.

XI

On Planning

PLANNING already has been defined, in the previous chapter, as the act of separating the manual and mental parts of an operation, in order that some portion of the mental effort can be transferred to a preliminary, planning stage. This, of course, is not the conventional definition.

Simply because of individual differences in manual and mental capabilities, this particular kind of division of labor undoubtedly has been applied in one way or another as long as there has been organized effort. However, form and impetus to this kind of planning were first given by Frederick W. Taylor, in his proposals for functional foremanship.[1] Taylor named four kinds of bosses in the shop: gang bosses, speed bosses, inspectors, and repair bosses; and "four representatives of the planning department": order of work and route clerk, instruction card clerk, time and cost clerk, and shop disciplinarian.

In addition to the objective of seeking expertness through rather extreme specialization, Taylor's intention was to have the "thinking" part of production concentrated in the hands of the first two clerks. The order of work and route card clerk would plan the sequence of jobs and the machines to be used for each, and the instruction card clerk would describe exactly what was to be done and exactly

[1] Frederick W. Taylor, *Shop Management*. New York, American Society of Mechanical Engineers, 1903, and Harper & Brothers, 1911, 1947.

how the work should be carried out, in such a way as to require a minimum of mental effort and judgment on the part of operators. Indeed, it was expected by Taylor that introduction of functional foremanship would transform the rank and file into "men who are of small calibre and attainments."[2]

Taylor's functional foremen are not be be found anywhere in industry today—for that matter there was no complete installation even when he was alive—but "planning departments" have caught on, and exist in organizations of many kinds. The economic reason for their existence is simple: the cost of planning and execution done separately in many instances is less than the cost of planning and execution done together.

This is so, not only because separation permits downgrading operators to men of "small calibre and attainments," but also because of the proficiencies gained by specialization, in the manner described by Adam Smith. It is a plain fact, verifiable by observation, that workmen, even of large calibre and attainments, are slow and uncertain problem solvers, when they encounter need for planning during the performance of an operation. And, when the operation uses a machine or some other capital item, the cost of the pauses and hesitations accompanying on-the-job planning are compounded.

2

The separation and transfer of mental effort is exactly analogous to the transfer of skill and intelligence from men to machines that characterized the industrial revolution and

[2] Ibid., p. 105 (1947 edition).

continues to characterize the development of semi-automatic machines and processes. When Maudslay devised the lead screw and tool rest for the early metal-cutting lathe, the skill and dexterity of the operator to hold the tool and lead it into the work were taken away from him and embodied in the machine. When Spencer conceived and added his "brain wheel," similar parts of the work—this time chiefly mental requirements—were removed from the operator and transferred to the machine. Innovations of these kinds have continued to appear, until now an experimental machine is capable of cutting metal to desired shapes in three dimensions, actuated by a punched tape and without need for an operator of conventional kind.

The introduction of planning in order to separate and transfer mental effort is quite similar to these familiar mechanical developments, except that planning is less spectacular, perhaps less well understood by administrators, and involves separation and transfer from man to man, rather than from man to machine.

Economically, the analogy also is exact. Introduction of the lead screw and tool rest made necessary a more expensive machine which could be run by a less expensive man. Through faster and more uniform output, this yielded a lower cost of goods produced. The brain wheel required a still more expensive machine and a still less expensive man and again cut the cost of goods produced. The tape-controlled modern colossus will require very large investment but apparently no man at all. In each case the cost of goods after innovation is less than the cost before and this may be expressed symbolically as follows:

$$\frac{M_2 + L_2}{N_2} < \frac{M_1 + L_1}{N_1}$$

where M_1 and M_2 respectively represent before and after machine investment costs, with $M_2 > M_1$; L_1 and L_2 before and after labor costs, with $L_2 < L_1$; and N_1 and N_2 quantities of goods produced. Usually $N_2 > N_1$ but this is not an essential condition; the basic inequality may hold for the same or smaller volume produced.

Just the same kind of inequality can be written for the introduction of planning, thus:

$$\frac{P + O}{N_2} < \frac{C}{N_1}$$

where P is the cost of *separate* planning, O is the cost of *separate* performance, and C is the cost of planning and performance done *together*. As in the case of new machines, a relatively higher priced man is needed for the now separated planning and a lower priced man for the remaining separate performance, but as much gain derives from greater proficiency through specialization as from this source. Also as before, N_2 may be greater than N_1 but this is not a necessary condition.

Inequalities such as these, expressed differently but essentially similar, have been used countless times to appraise the possibilities of new technology and new methods. Capital costs of a new venture are assessed, the probable labor cost is forecast, the market is weighed, and the results of this appraisal are compared with similar data for the current situation. If the comparison is sufficiently favorable to the new way, either in reduced cost of product or service, improved performance or quality, greater profit, or in sufficiently brief "pay-out" time, the innovation is adopted. If not, it is deferred or abandoned.

This kind of procedure is familiar to every administrator and merits exposition here only to emphasize what is much less familiar: that the potential of separating manual from mental labor offers possibilities of technological advance which are often not realized.

3

This, and other points yet to be made, may be illustrated by an example.

The pages of this book were printed from type, "made-up" into pages like this one and "imposed" for press in "forms." The work of "imposition" is performed by skilled compositors who lay the desired pages out on large flat-topped tables called "stones." (Years ago these tables were made of slate-like material ground to a smooth finish; hence the name stones. Now such tables have steel tops but compositors doing such work still are called "stone men.")

Before the planning changes to be described were introduced, the stone men would be given a set of page proof, margin specifications for type pages of standard size for the book to be printed, the trimmed size, the size paper to be used on press, and an instruction that the job was to be printed in forms of 32 or 16 pages, with added details covering the smaller forms needed to round out the number of pages in the job. Using this information, the stone man would select from the proof the pages needed for the first "white form" (e.g., pages 1, 4, 5, 8, 9, 12, 13, 16, 17, 20, 21, 24, 25, 28, 29, and 32), procure them from their storage locations, and lay them on the stone in such an arrangement that when "backed-up" by pages 2, 3, 6, 7, etc. all would fold in correct order of pagination.

To do this the stone man had to be thoroughly familiar with all of the many kinds of folding layouts, for page 1 can be placed in many different positions and the placing thereof literally determines where all of the other pages in the job will go. Obviously page 2 must be placed in the back-up form so as to follow page 1 in the finished book, and pages 33, 65, etc., as the initial pages of successive signatures, must correspond in position to page 1, in order that the folding pattern may be consistent throughout.

To say that the operators consciously pondered these matters on each form handled would be a gross exaggeration; much of what they did fell into a common, routine pattern. But whenever the unusual occurred, as it did fairly often, thought and decision were required and each man had to know many layouts of many different kinds.

Much more difficult problems were presented by type pages of nonstandard size. Once the desired pages had been assembled on the stone in correct printing and folding arrangement, the stone man had to place around them a hollow-square steel frame called a "chase" (see fig. 6, page 116) and then space the pages relative to the frame itself, to its center bars, and to other pages in such a way that each would appear in the finished work in a position artistically pleasing to the eye and taste of the customer and reader. This was simple enough for type pages of standard size, these being governed by the given margin specifications, but was more difficult for oversize and undersize pages (see, for example, the front matter pages of this book).

For each of these the stone man had to make a calculation and follow a conventional rule. If a page was wider than standard, he diminished the bind margin and front margin each by half of the excess. If a page was longer than standard by one or two lines and carried a running head, he took all of the excess from the standard foot margin, so that running head alignment would be preserved on facing pages. If there was no running head, or if the excess was three lines or more, he diminished the standard head and foot margins by half of the difference, just as described for excess width.

Practice permitted most such moves to be made without hesitation and the problem was not as complex in most cases as it sounds here. Yet it was complex enough to result in serious delays, inconsistencies within a job, and occasional spoilage requiring re-work. Observe, for example, that the bind margin to the fold is less here than the front margin, and the head margin is less than the foot. Application of the halving rule to very large pages would cause them to print off the paper into the trim at the top and into the fold at the bind when there would still be white space at foot and front for the amount of oversize.

In such extreme cases, and in other instances where type page sizes would vary from page to page, planning by the operators themselves was both hesitant and poor. Often imposition would be carried out to the best of the stone man's ability but with the comfortable knowledge that verification would be made on press by the hand folding and checking of the first press sheet. When this had been done, out-of-position pages could be moved and checked again, and then again and again if necessary. During this essential precautionary process no thought was given to the inaccuracies of hand folding and little more to the long delays to expensive machines caused by these inspection procedures.

Planning, as it has been defined in this chapter, was introduced for this operation as indicated in Fig. 6. By this change all of the decisions just described were taken away from the stone men and transferred to the planning department. Each form now goes to the stones with a diagram which specifies the layout and position of each page. Margin adjustments for oversize pages are not left to the operators but are given as shown for page 11 in the illustration. No longer is it necessary to be fearful of printing in the trim or on a fold, or to hold a press for a cumbersome and inaccurate hand-folded OK.

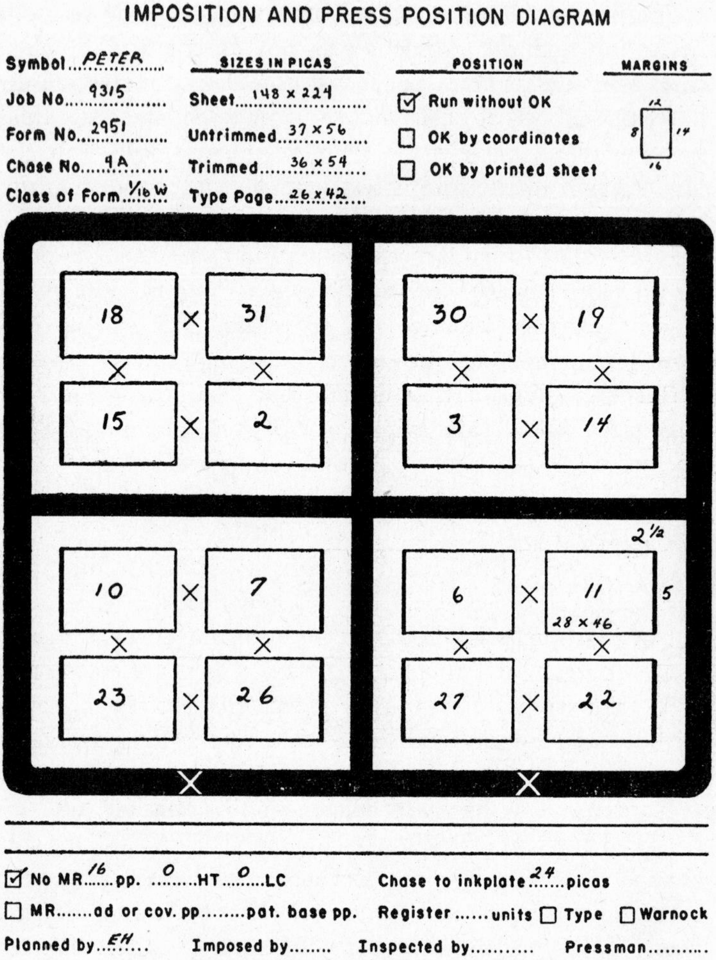

IMPOSITION AND PRESS POSITION DIAGRAM

Symbol ...PETER...	SIZES IN PICAS	POSITION	MARGINS
Job No...9315...	Sheet...148 × 224...	☑ Run without OK	
Form No...2951...	Untrimmed...37 × 56...	☐ OK by coordinates	
Chase No...4A...	Trimmed...36 × 54...	☐ OK by printed sheet	
Class of Form...1/16 W...	Type Page...26 × 42...		

☑ No MR...16...pp. ...0...HT ...0...LC   Chase to inkplate...24...picas
☐ MR...ad or cov. pp...pat. base pp.   Register ...units ☐ Type ☐ Warnock
Planned by...EH...   Imposed by...   Inspected by...   Pressman...

Fig. 6. Planning technique used in a printing operation.

These and other changes too extensive for discussion here had dramatic effect upon the economy of the operation. Imposition that formerly required the services of seven stone men came to be done with three, press foremen were relieved of folding and checking a very large number of press sheets, and delays to machines were reduced to a fraction of their former magnitude.

Of course, not all of this was net gain. The introduction of planning required staff engineering services to conceive, test, and introduce the change. The preparation of imposition diagrams in the planning department requires the part-time services of two people. Press foremen are salaried personnel and relieving them of routine duties does not at once or directly reflect a saving in cost. But despite these elements of expense, the net gain remained very large. From this example, we can repeat the inequality stated on page 112:

$$\frac{P + O}{N_2} < \frac{C}{N_1},$$

and say as a reasonable generalization that planning as a concept offers economic attractions to administrators.

4

Having said this, it is now necessary to hedge and to say that the foregoing inequality and its analogue given on page 111 are incomplete. The picture for planning and for technological change is not as favorable as thus far indicated. There are important elements of cost not included in either formula.

With respect to the inequality stated just above, there is one obvious omission: the engineering costs associated with conceiving, developing, and instituting the planning technique. This element is comparable to the term M_2 in the previously stated inequality, which allowed for the capital costs associated with new machine investment.

However, the missing element of cost to be discussed here

is not omitted just from the inequality for planning; it is missing from *both* of the formulas.

Introduction of the planning concept to the operation of imposition resulted in a substantial saving. Three stone men did the work formerly carried out by seven, these three could be "men of small calibre and attainments," as specified by Taylor, and the quotient

$$\frac{E + P + O}{N_2}$$

(with E = the cost of engineering development) was much lower than the former unit cost represented by C/N_1.

But what about the four stone men displaced by the change? And what about the three stone men remaining on the job? Obviously, part of the cost of the change has been borne by them.

Conventionally, these familiar questions are explained away by various equally familiar responses. The traditional rationalization is to say that the four displaced men are not displaced at all, except perhaps temporarily. This explanation says in effect that there is no such thing as technological unemployment; technological advances *make* jobs through cost reduction, price reduction, elastic markets, and better living standards. Compare employment today in the mechanized shoe industry with that of the days when shoes were sewn by hand. Do the same thing for textiles, wagons and automobiles, electric bulbs and candles, and the result will be the same. Adjust for population, allow for some inelastic markets, and still one can say that technology does not destroy jobs, it creates them.

This explanation *is* a rationalization, and sometimes a self-justifying one, simply because the particular John Does and Richard Roes who were removed from the imposition operation were, in fact, displaced. Markets are neither perfectly nor instantly elastic and, even if impositon comes ultimately to require more than the original force of seven, the new men are not likely to be the same persons.

This desirable recognition of the individual worker often is accompanied by the rationalization that the men displaced from imposition are given employment elsewhere, in this case in the composing room at their going wages. Hence the new method causes no displacement and the operators bear no cost.

Admittedly, this kind of solution is sometimes the best that can be done but it is still not a perfect solution. It is a mistake—very often made—to assume that this procedure removes all cost from the transferred operators. They may suffer no monetary loss but they are almost certain to experience insecurity from the threats posed by the new development, discomfort from the requirements of new habit formation, and loss of status in their new environment. These may be only transitory feelings but they are not without cost.

The same kinds of things may be said of the three men still needed for the job. Various possibilities may be stated. Now, with a diagram for each form, the job needs only "men of small calibre and attainments." Perhaps—the threat certainly exists—the company will see fit to replace the skilled men with others less skilled and less costly. Or they may continue to use the experienced large calibre men for the now small calibre job, and offer small calibre wages for it. More generously, they may keep three of the original crew on the job at no reduction in wages, or, finally, they may even pay higher wages for the simplified tasks, as a way of sharing gains from the improvement with the workers.

In every one of these cases, including the last, the affected workers bear part of the cost of transition. The stone man who remains on the job at secure higher wages has had his years of investment in skill and knowledge rendered completely obsolete. The layouts he once knew now are handed to him, the margins he once calculated now are specified, the problems he once overcame now are solved for him. Beside him he can see a boy, who once disassembled printed forms for remelting or storage, but who now can impose from a diagram as well as the stone man.

Money can mitigate but not eradicate costs such as these. A personal anecdote will serve to make the point. In another part of this same rather comprehensive engineering development, improved control of certain critical dimensions eliminated craft attributes of a skilled job, just as had been done on the stones. Conscious of the impact of the change upon the operators, we had promised full-time, stable employment and a monetary share in the gains achieved. Both of these objectives had been realized to the satisfaction of the management, the engineers, and, we thought, the men.

Soon after the changes had been made, the receptionist called one morning to say that one of the midnight shift operators, George K—, was in the front office and wanted to see me. Since he had finished work several hours before, at 7 A.M., this was puzzling but I went down and saw, as anyone could, that George was drunk. We went into a conference room and George himself at once said that he was drunk, that he had been drinking since quitting time in order to screw up his courage to return to the plant to tell me off.

He did just that but it soon became clear that what had happened in the department was the focus of his resentment. Skills that he had possessed through years of experience now were useless to him. It did not matter—at least not enough —that he received better wages and enjoyed job security;

what hurt was the obsolescence of those parts of his job that had been satisfying to him, that paid off in creativeness, that set him above and apart from the young beginners who could not do the things he could. Now the satisfactions and the distinction of superior status were gone and the extra money did not compensate for those losses.

The story would not be complete without reporting that K— soon thereafter led a union organizing drive in his department and missed success by just one vote. After that he left for another job, where his skill and status still could be enjoyed. I have not seen him since but he has my respect and I will not forget the hurt he caused me. It is not pleasant to think that a fellow-worker must get drunk to get the courage to talk plainly.

George K— felt as he did because part of the cost of the new method was being borne by him, in the loss of valued skill and satisfaction—and he saw no commensurate way to recover that loss. Thus, technological transition *always* is accompanied by social cost and this is the element that is missing from both of the inequalities. They should read

$$\frac{M_2 + L_2 + S}{N_2} < \frac{M_1 + L_1}{N_1}$$

and

$$\frac{E + P + O + S}{N_2} < \frac{C}{N_1},$$

if investment in change is to be made.

5

No doubt this argument for inclusion of social cost is familiar enough, perhaps even hackneyed, yet the conviction remains that reiterated emphasis is deserved. The evaluation of S is exceedingly difficult but this does not excuse administrators from slighting or ignoring it. Evaluation, however approximate, is not merely considerate or humane; because humanity has value, the term is part of the decision-making calculation in the full economic sense. The administrator who ignores this fact is not wisely doing his job.

Part of the difficulty attending the evaluation of social cost is that the term S is really an aggregate function consisting of a multitude of small s's, many of them reaching back into the general history of relationships in organizations, some of them deriving from the history of the instant organization itself, and some of them dependent upon individual behavior and individual differences. Today's foreman, or sergeant, or bureau chief, or church elder, or dean is to his subordinates and associates not only himself as a person but also the partial image of all of his respective predecessors, in all similar organizations, as well as in his own. The introduction of planning to imposition was not a technological change *in vacuo*, it was also in the image of the tool rest and lead screw, the brain wheel, the power loom and the punched tape. George K— was more than just a pressman, he was also in the image of the feudal serf, the degraded worker of the Industrial Revolution, the traditional victim of greedy bosses, the pawn of the capitalists. These are clichés, to be sure; perhaps they have become so because they have the right connotations for people like George K—. Perhaps he thought of himself in these terms or in others like them. We do not know. We know that he was motivated to protest because of lack of satisfaction and lost status in his work but we do not know—nor did he—to what extent his actions were influenced by forces such as these.

Thus complete or precise assessment of the social cost of

change is impossible. We can only say that social cost *always* accompanies technological change and offers virtuous admonitions to administrators for its evaluation and minimization:

1. Perceive that it does and will exist and refrain from self-justifying rationalization.

2. Maximize communication and candor to those who will be affected. This is a pious statement but an important one.

3. Insofar as it is possible to do so, preserve the security and status of those who are threatened by the change. Do not indulge in the phony rationalization that technological change makes jobs. It does but not for the same people.

4. Preserve, so far as possible, those ingredients of work which contribute to satisfaction. And do not indulge in another phony rationalization: that workers like monotony.

5. When preservation of elements contributing to satisfaction is not possible, seek to find substitutes. Participation in the development itself is one such substitute; enhanced participation in the enterprise as a whole is another.

6. Recognize that money alone cannot buy off social cost *in toto*. Be "selfishly generous" in sharing the gains from technology but do not assume that this is *the* solution. The concept of "economic man" has been exploded.

7. Be humane because humanity has value, not because being humane is comforting to the conscience. This is an economic calculation, not uplift.

6

This essay set out to show that the division of manual and mental labor, here called planning, is a concept that often is overlooked or not understood by administrators. To this primary argument has been added strong emphasis upon social cost as an inevitable part of the planning concept.

It is fair to ask why this secondary emphasis has been so strong, perhaps too strong. I do not know but suspect that an innate conviction is responsible, namely, that one of the evils of modern society is too much worship of organizations and of the god of efficiency, and too little reverence for the creative satisfactions of work and for the individuals who perform it.

XII

On the Resolution of Conflict

THE first case history presented in chapters II, III, and IV described a conflict situation in which keyboard operators demanded a change in time standards deemed by them to be unfair. In discussing this case it was pointed out that the actions taken resulted in a better situation for *both* of the disputants. Training, maintenance, and improved scheduling yielded better wages to the operators and substantial operating economies to management. Neither party dominated the other and there was no yielding by either in the way of compromise.

The conflict, it was said then, was *integrated* in the manner described by Mary Parker Follett in her collected papers.[1]

Miss Follett defines conflict as any difference between two persons or parties and says that such differences may be resolved by the three means already referred to: by *domination*, by *compromise*, or by *integration*. Domination and compromise are such familiar things in everyday living as to require little exploration here. The dominant person or party wins and the dominated person or party loses, when this way of resolution is employed. With compromise there is no decisive victory or defeat, instead there is

---

[1] Henry C. Metcalf, and L. Urwick (Eds.), *Dynamic Administration, The Collected Papers of Mary Parker Follett*. New York: Harper & Brothers, 1940.

division; each gives up part of what was wanted in order to keep a share.

The resolution of conflicts by these means has the unfortunate attribute of leaving the seeds of future conflict in fertile soil. He who dominates may be quite satisfied with his solution but not he who is dominated. He has swallowed the bitter pill of subjugation and will be motivated to challenge his oppressor at the first new opportunity. Compromise diminishes the bitterness by dividing the frustration in some proportion between those who are at odds. But, since each gives up something of what was wanted, frustration is still present to contribute to and aggravate future differences.

Integration, as has been said already, is resolution of conflict by means which yield gain to both of the disputants. The conflict itself is made to work *for* those in dispute, to yield a result which is better than that which existed before the dispute occurred.

Obviously, integration is not always possible. Many conflicts, by their very nature, do not permit this kind of resolution. Many more do but fail of integration because of human frailty. If either of two disputants is hell-bent upon dominating the other, integration is not possible. If either mistrusts the other, integration is not possible. If neither thinks of this means, integration will not result. If one thinks of integration but does not broach the idea, or broaches it and has it rejected, there will be none. It takes two to integrate a conflict. One may lead and propose but his opponent must understand and respond in kind, or there will be no integration.

These restrictions are much more severe than is apparent on casual reading. Ignorance of the concept of integration is widespread. Mistrust between those in conflict often is too deep to permit either disputant to lower his guard to make integration possible. And, above all, the desire to dominate is so very strong in all of us as to put integration beyond our reach. We lack the wisdom and the strength to sacrifice the will to win, the desire for victory, for the larger but less personal gains of integration.

None of this is in the least original but is merely a statement of Miss Follett's ideas in my own words. The examples which follow, however, are mine. The keyboard conflict already described was a narrative of successful integration; those which follow were regrettably in the realm of "might have been," the first because of ignorance and the second because of mistrust and desire to dominate. Both, I hope, will reveal not only the opportunities which were missed but the very great significance of Miss Follett's concept to those in administration.

2

Several years ago I served as arbitrator for a company and a labor union who enjoyed the best labor-management relationship I have yet encountered. Mutual regard and respect between executives of the company and officials of the union were high. Each party quite obviously trusted the other. There was abundant and agreeable intercommunication between them. When grievances were carried to arbitration, which was seldom, hearings were marked by good will and informality and were often preceded by the statement, "This is an honest difference of opinion which we want you to resolve." In short, conditions here were right for the integration of conflict.

The company, a manufacturer of consumer goods, had been plagued by theft in one of its plants. This was first revealed by an agent of the trucking firm employed to make deliveries from the company warehouse; he disclosed that one or two of their drivers had been suspected of making unauthorized deliveries and proposed that private detectives be hired to trail the suspects. This was done, the suspicion was verified, and the guilty truck drivers were discharged and, perhaps—I do not know—prosecuted. These drivers were not employees of the company but there had to be an inside accomplice to enable them to steal as they had been doing.

Following this revelation, a physical inventory disclosed a shortage of more than 800 cases of product, a loss so serious as to lead to stringent security measures. A warehouse superintendent of long experience was brought from another plant and charged with the duty of eliminating theft. He called the warehouse crew to meetings. He warned them that taking even a single item, much less a case, would lead to instant discharge. He instituted spot recounts of loaded vehicles without warning. He particularly admonished those employees whom he suspected had collaborated with the guilty drivers but he could not establish their guilt.

These events in the warehouse proper were accompanied by a plant-wide campaign as well. In this the company wisely enlisted the aid of the union and the union responded. Officers held meetings with department stewards and discussed the problem and there was forthright publicity in the form of articles and editorials in the union newspaper. One might surmise a certain degree of rank-and-file indifference in areas of the plant where theft was not feasible and a certain lack of militance and vigor in the union's efforts, but they were sincere. It was the company's problem but the union wanted to help.

During these months an employee of about three year's

service—then the age of the plant—worked in the process department of the company and was the department steward for the union. This employee, who will be called Rollins, had as steward attended union meetings where stealing was discussed but one may suppose that the matter was then of no special concern to him, because stealing was not a problem in his department.

On a previous occasion, long before stealing had become an issue, Rollins had served as vacation relief in the warehouse, in the capacity of yardmaster, directing the railroad switch crew in the movement of freight cars of inbound raw materials and outbound finished goods. In this temporary capacity he had acquitted himself well and apparently liked the job too, for he asked for permanent transfer from process to warehouse when an opening came early in the summer after the theft discovery. Rollins, as I say, bid for the yardmaster job and got it at a time when the theft episode was a memory but still a very fresh one. He was not in the audience when the new superintendent laid down the law to the warehouse crew but he missed those stern admonitions by only a month or two.

One of Rollins's friends among the employees and in the union was Leith, who had at one time worked as crewman for a railroad—not the one serving the plant but another in the area. Leith in casual conversations had told Rollins of practices of polite bribery—he didn't call it that—which went on between railroad switch crews and the plants they served. To insure that the railroad men would be accommodating they would be given a ham by a packing house, ice cream by a dairy, beer by a brewery, and so on. According to Leith's testimony at the arbitration hearing, he had told Rollins of this in such a way as to convey that this sort of thing was accepted practice.

At the time of his transfer back to the yardmaster's job,

Rollins was turned over to a senior warehouse employee for more thorough training than the two week's prior duty had afforded and, at the end of two weeks or so of instruction, was assigned to the A shift, to work on his own from midnight to 8 a.m.

According to Rollins's own testimony, his brief refresher training was not quite adequate and he made a mistake or two during his first week on the midnight shift, placing cars where they did not belong, so that the switch crew had to make extra moves, for which Rollins's company should have had to pay. He escaped getting into trouble, however, because the switch crew made the extra moves but did not enter them on the railroad charge sheet. This was cheating the railroad of legitimate income, of course, but it did place Rollins under obligation to the switchmen.

Not long after his assignment to the A shift, again according to Rollins's testimony, one of the switchmen asked him point blank for a case of company product and Rollins, feeling obligated, carried a case out of the warehouse into an empty box car standing at the loading platform. The plant itself was surrounded by a wire fence, with the main gate under guard, but the tracks came into the area in a remote corner where there was no guard or watchman. The general idea was to take the case out of the yard in the empty box car when the engine pulled outbound cars away to the main line.

Unfortunately for Rollins, the C shift foreman had worked later than his usual midnight quitting time and, when Rollins carried the case across the loading dock at about 12:50 a.m., he was seen under the platform lights by the foreman, who was then in his automobile in the parking lot outside the fence. As soon as he saw Rollins, the foreman left his car and ran through the main gate, calling the guard to follow as he ran toward the loading dock. He got there almost as soon as Rollins emerged from the boxcar, accosted him, and required him to replace the case in the warehouse. He expressed surprise and shock at Rollins's action but meted out no discipline at the time. The foreman then went home and Rollins continued on the job. The guard returned to the gate-house and entered the incident upon his log sheet, as required by company regulations.

The next morning the company personnel officer routinely received and reviewed this log and from it learned of the attempted theft. He called the foreman by telephone, heard his account of the affair, and suspended Rollins by telegram (he had no telephone), pending a disciplinary hearing. The contract between the company and union stipulated that discharge could not be invoked until such a hearing had been held before a board consisting of company executives not directly concerned with supervision of the accused. In this instance, as I recall this detail, the board consisted of the director of research, the controller, and the sales manager.

At this hearing Rollins was present and was supported by the union president, who pleaded on his behalf but to no avail. The board voted to discharge Rollins and this was done. Thereupon the union, as privileged by the contract, requested arbitration before an impartial umpire, a role which then was filled by me.

Aside from an abortive attempt by the union to show that company executives had created an atmosphere of laxity toward company products by their freedom with them, the arbitration hearing disclosed the situation substantially as I have narrated it here. Rollins made an excellent witness in his own behalf; he was a clean-cut, forthright, and manly young fellow; his work history was of the very best; his support from union officers and fellow workers, themselves persons of integrity, was warm and staunch. Clearly, he was not a thief in any sense of habit or personal gain. Curiously, the railroad switch crew were neither identified nor heard from, I suppose because of possible embarrassment to the railroad and self-incrimination of the switchmen. Thus, Rollins's story that he was giving the case to them went unsupported but there was no reason to doubt this explanation.

However, he had appropriated a case of company product and was caught in the very act. Furthermore, he did this on the heels of serious, large-scale thefts, which he had known about as process department steward. To do what he did as a green employee in the warehouse, when he must or should have known of company vigilance, was, in the kindest words, incredibly foolish. The company, proceeding judiciously and legally at every step, had established guilt and decided upon discharge. Sustaining this action was the only course open to the arbitrator and such an award was duly made.

Thus, the company had its way and "won" the conflict by a process of domination. To be sure, it was a nice kind of domination, accompanied by a final quasi-judicial procedure, but still the company won and the incident was closed. No doubt Rollins felt a degree of unhappiness that would color his attitude toward his next employer and no doubt the union had feelings too that would color their future relations with the company. These were necessary costs in settlement of the conflict.

But were they? Having won, was there any action available to the company which would have mitigated these losses and accomplished a net gain?

The answer is to be found in Victor Hugo's *Les Miserables*, in the action of the Bishop of Digne, who told the arresting officers that Jean Valjean had been given the silver which he had in reality stolen. The salutary effect of this extraordinary action upon Jean Valjean could have been duplicated in the case of Rollins, *if company executives had been wise enough to restore Rollins to his job after winning the arbitration award*.

By such an act of forgiveness, only possible after winning the arbitration award, the company would have bound Rollins's loyalty and his honesty to them with hoops of steel. He was not a thief of the same stripe as those who had mulcted the company of 800 cases, he was only a foolish man, much more like the Jean Valjean who had been chained to a galley oar for stealing a loaf of bread. No one can say with certainty how he would have responded to magnanimity but the potential gain was clearly worth the risk.

By such an act of forgiveness the company would have bound the union and its people to them in the same way. The union opposed theft, as any honest outfit would, but with Rollins returned to his job it is more than just a fair bet that their regard for company goods and company property would have been transformed from a kind of tacit "editorial support" to militant protection.

Integration by this means was thought of, I might add, by the director of labor relations from the central office of the company. I learned this much later, on an occasion when I had the chance to tell him the views expressed here. After winning the award, he had favored the reinstatement of Rollins himself but felt, as I did, that such an action must come spontaneously and sincerely from the local people and not as a suggestion or seeming directive from higher authority.

And so the potential gains were lost in an almost ideal

climate for their attainment. "The saddest words of tongue or pen . . . ."

3

The local people who could have integrated the Rollins conflict failed to do so, not because they lacked either good will or acumen, but because of ignorance of the concept. This is simply my opinion, of course, as is the preliminary statement that the following case could not be integrated because each party was so determined to have its own way, to dominate the other, to "spit in the other's eye," as to be blinded completely to the real issue.

This is a narrative of arbitration too, between a large manufacturer of ball bearings and a labor union. Here there appeared to be little regard between company and union people. Grievances were carried to arbitration as often as they were settled by mutual agreement. Formality characterized the hearing. Militance and antipathy tainted the atmosphere throughout. Integration would have been impossible, even if thought of; this case will serve only to show the lengths to which antagonistic human beings will go to win over an adversary.

There were employed in the company a number of girls who were engaged in the visual inspection of ball bearings. They performed this operation in one of two ways: by machine or on trays. The machines in question did not actually inspect the balls but merely served to pass them before the inspectress in such a way that she could visually examine each one and extract and discard defectives with a small pencil-like magnet. Tray inspection, the other method used, required the girl to scoop the bearings into a felt-lined tray, tilt the tray back and forth, causing the balls to roll to and fro over the felt, examine them, and extract the defectives with a magnet. The good bearings would be put into a container for the next operation and the defectives discarded as scrap.

Each inspectress worked under a wage incentive plan which provided for the payment of wages in proportion to the number of balls inspected. There were time standards for bearings of each diameter and these standards allowed a specified number of minutes per pound for each size. These allowances would be higher for the small diameters, with more balls per pound, than for the larger sizes, with fewer per pound. The net effect was to establish a relationship by which earnings were proportional to the number of balls examined. It should be added that each inspectress had a base hourly wage rate and that earnings could not fall below the product of this rate times the hours worked.

These relationships may be summarized mathematically as:

$$E_{min} = R \times H$$

for minimum earnings (usually called "base pay") and

$$E_I = f(N)$$

for incentive earnings, with

E_{min} = Minimum earnings,
E_I = Incentive earnings,
R = Hourly base wage rate,
H = Hours worked,
N = Number of ball bearings inspected.

To carry out her job each inspectress was instructed to look for and eradicate flaws which were referred to as "flats," "surface checks," and something called "hair-lap," a hair-like deficiency named for the lapping machines which were the source of this particular defect. These three classes of defects were not equally easy to see; large flats were fairly obvious, surface checks or cracks somewhat less so, and hair-lap still harder to discern. Moreover, the total number of balls examined obviously would be dependent upon the number of defectives of any kind found, because each such defective required a pause for removal and disposal with the magnet.

Thus, the equation $E = f(N)$ is a true representation of the operation only when the number of rejects and the qualitative character of the defects happen to be the same as in the sample upon which the time allowances originally were based. Let an inspectress encounter a lot with a higher percentage of rejects than allowed for in the time standards, or with more difficult defects to detect, and her earnings would fall. Let the overall quality of a given lot be better than the average, and incentive earnings would rise, assuming comparable operator effort in each instance.

In such a wage incentive situation inspectresses would be motivated in various ways. In the first place they would be seriously tempted to pass a given lot without inspecting them at all, claiming credit and wages for the poundage involved and letting the defectives be discovered, if at all, at some subsequent time. Or they would give the bearings only a quick cursory examination. However, the company was on to this rather obvious possibility and provided for it by a system of reinspection by non-incentive inspectresses called "checkers." Each lot examined by an incentive inspectress went to a checker, who randomly reinspected 20 per cent of it. If more than an allowed per cent defective was found in this random sample, the whole lot went back to the original inspectress to be done over on her "own time," without incentive compensation.

This kind of control maintained outgoing quality all right, but did not satisfy the operators when defectives were numerous or hard to see. From the outset inspectresses complained vociferously when they encountered a bad lot and, of course, said nothing when quality was above average, because this was to their benefit.

The company met these complaints by three successive relaxations of the inspection time standards. They called these relaxations "demerit sheets" and in effect they established percentages of defectives at or above which an inspectress would be granted an "off-standard condition," which will be explained in a moment. The first demerit sheet was prepared and posted by the company but the complaints continued as loudly as before and the company thereupon drafted and put into effect a more liberal version. When this did not pacify the inspection group, a third, still more liberal sheet was prepared but this time the company was wary; they insisted that union officials sign this third document as acceptable to them.

Under this arrangement an inspectress would start work upon a given lot and, if she came to feel that defectives were running too high, she would call the foreman. Apparently this happened more often than not. The foreman would come to the girl's machine or tray, look at what she had done, and perhaps inspect a sample himself. If the number of defectives found by this means was higher than the number specified on the demerit sheet, the foreman, as an official act, would permit the lot to be done as an off-standard condition.

Off-standard conditions were defined in the collective agreement as, "Jobs which deviate from the standard operating specifications and which require more time than the standard unit time allowed." The contract further provided that operators on off-standard conditions should be paid 120 per cent of base pay as a minimum. This was a floor and not a ceiling, for an operator still could earn more than 120 per cent of base pay, if she produced at faster than this pace.

Under these conditions the inspectresses had everything to gain and nothing to lose by yelling for the foreman to check the demerit sheet. If he said no, they were no worse off. If he said yes, their guaranteed minimum was at once boosted to $1.20 \times R \times H$, without in the least inhibiting their chance at higher incentive wages.

It is easy to imagine what happened. A girl would call for the foreman and in a very large number of cases be permitted the sought-for off-standard condition. Then, if her experience and sensitivity to pace told her that she could beat 120 per cent of base pay, she continued to strive for the incentive, secure in her knowledge that the worst that could happen would still yield 120 per cent of base wages. If, on the other hand, she perceived that 120 per cent efficiency was out of reach altogether, she could relax and take her own sweet time, again knowing that 120 per cent was guaranteed for that lot of bearings. The sensitivity of incentive workers to that pace which will yield a desired rate of pay, I should add, is at least as acute as an orchestra conductor's sensitivity to the right tempo for a symphony. Workers have almost uncanny perception of matters so vital to their welfare.

At the hearing, company representatives gave eloquent testimony on this point by offering statistics to show that inspection efficiencies, that is, the ratios of standard times allowed to actual times taken, averaged only 25 per cent when girls were working under off-standard conditions. This means that they were taking four times as long to inspect these lots as the pace necessary to earn minimum base pay on measured incentive work. And for this snail-like tempo they were guaranteed 120 per cent, almost five times their incentive entitlement.

This enormously significant fact was introduced into the hearing more or less incidentally; it was not the stated issue of the case. The dispute itself centered about a change in method introduced by the company and indicated by the diagram in Fig. 7. In the size range ¼ to ⅜ inch original time standards had been set as indicated by the left half of the figure. Bearings first were put through "Machine Junk Inspection" for the purpose of eradicating obvious defectives, and then were subjected to a statistical sampling plan, whereby only out-of-control lots went to the incentive inspectresses for 100 per cent examination.

In this size range the company proposed to eliminate junk inspection, leaving the sequence of operations as portrayed beneath the dotted line. The union objected on the ground that inspectresses now would have additional defectives to find and remove, these being the rejects formerly extracted during junk inspection. They asked that the standards be withdrawn. The significance of this demand will be explained in a moment.

In the size range 13⁄32 to ½ inch all of the balls previously had been given 100 per cent inspection by the incentive operators, as shown in the right half of Fig. 7. For these sizes the company proposed to introduce statistical sampling inspection in an operation cycle just like that under the dotted line on the left side of the chart. To this the union also objected, this time on the ground that now inspectresses would receive for 100 per cent inspection only lots which had been rejected by the sampling plan as out-of-control. Since the original time standards presumably

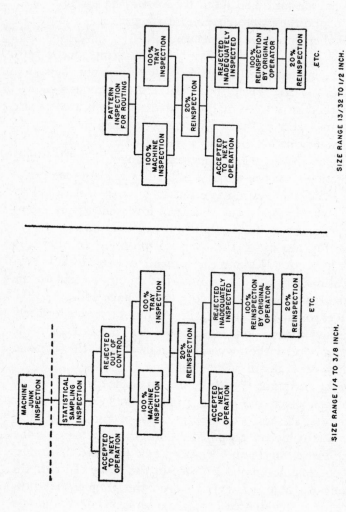

Fig. 7. Inspection process charts.

represented averages of all lots, good and bad, this change, so the union argued, would work to the girls' disadvantage. They asked that these standards be withdrawn too.

This demand was made because the contract provided for the withdrawal of standards which no longer measured performance and in such cases compensation was fixed at 130 per cent of base pay, regardless of the work pace of the inspectresses. Thus, the operators, already receiving a 120-plus guarantee each time they won an off-standard condition, now were asking for an additional ten points for all work in the full size range ¼ to ½ inch. (Incidentally, this size range is not so small as it appears, because diameters vary by small increments. There are many sizes between ¼ and ½ inch.)

At first glance, it is easy to see why the union made its demand and why the company opposed. The union wanted a guarantee of more money and the company resisted the increase. But this was a superficial and erroneous view on the part of the company. By their own admission, they were already paying through the nose because of the inadequate standards, for each time a girl worked off-standard and knew she couldn't hit above 120 per cent, she slowed down to a crawl and worked at 25 per cent efficiency for 120 per cent wages. The best action available to the company was the very withdrawal demanded by the union, because they could then set new, functionally accurate time-standards which would at one fell swoop, so to speak, wash out demerit sheets, off-standard conditions, red tape, soldiering, and the cost of high wages for low performance. They could, in short, have sought an integrated solution, one that would have yielded net gains to both of the parties in conflict.

To those unfamiliar with time standards and incentive

systems, this case may seem technically complex and the issue obscure but to those who have rubbed shoulders with incentive plans, the issue will be clear, as it should have been to the parties involved. Why then did the company so militantly oppose that which was in their own interest? Even if company people were ignorant of the concept of integration—which they were, I'm sure—why would they still be so blind? The answer, I think, is that they were blinded by antagonism to the union and, to be fair, the union was equally blinded by antagonism to the company. Under such conditions objectivity and equity fly out the window and each party engages in combat for the sole purpose of winning a victory over an adversary. Under such conditions integration has no chance whatever.

The standards were ordered withdrawn by the arbitration award; this, to be sure, gave the company the chance to set new time allowances but in no sense achieved integration.

4

A colleague, before whom I once narrated this case in a seminar, said in discussion that Miss Follett's concept of integration had been described by the philosopher Hegel, who called it "concrescence." By whatever name it is called, it is a concept of importance to administrators, requiring of them a higher order of perception, intelligence, and self-discipline than the more usual and more pedestrian techniques of domination and compromise.

My commentator-colleague also pointed out that integrated solutions to conflicts always require that one or the other disputant give up something of value to attain the desired end. In view of the definition that integration yields a net gain to *both* of those in conflict, this is more subtle and perhaps paradoxical.

What was given up in the keyboard case? By the Bishop of Digne? What would company executives have surrendered in reinstating Rollins to his job? What would have been lost if the standards had been withdrawn as a willing, voluntary act? The answer in each case appears to be authority, the right to say what the solution must be, the desire to dominate. Apparently, this is not a little thing to give up, if one may judge from the paucity of integrated solutions. Apparently executives, or at least a great many of them, do not have the power or the perception to see that authority is not really surrendered by integration, it only *seems* to be, and then only in a momentary sense.

The power and prestige of the Bishop of Digne were raised, not diminished, by his gift of silver to Jean Valjean. Executive relations with the keyboard operators were improved, not damaged, by seeking integration instead of "proving" that the standards were "right." Restoring Rollins to his job would have increased company authority, even while seeming to yield to the union's demand. And, in each of these cases, those seeming to sacrifice authority by yielding, by giving in, gain not only in the eyes of their opposites, but in their own eyes as well. Integration indeed does yield a net gain.

XIII

On Morale

MORALE may be defined as the degree to which organization goals and goals of the individuals who comprise organization are compatible, to such extent as these goals have common ground. Poor morale may be described accurately as a condition of incompatibility in individual and organization goals but, conversely, good morale requires more than compatibility alone. It also requires the individual pursuit of organization goals with enthusiasm and energy. Passive, apathetic, or indifferent acquiescence to organization goals can only describe a condition of indifferent morale.

Good morale further requires the individuals in organization to pursue organization goals with energy that is supplied voluntarily, because they *want to* as individuals, not because it is the wish of the boss, or through threat of punishment or promise of reward. If compulsion is exercised in a high morale situation, it comes at the time of indoctrination of new members into the organization, and it comes from all levels, not from administration alone. A new U. S. Marine does not behave "like a Marine" because of the Commandant's order but because he either wants to or will be made to by his fellow enlisted men and immediate superiors. A rookie New York Yankee does not "act like a Yankee" because Casey Stengel tells him to. He is likely to want to in the first place but, if he doesn't, he will be subjected to pressure and compulsion from his teammates. A Johns Hopkins medical student will behave in the same way and be exposed to the same forces.

Good morale, as exemplified by these organizations, always is accompanied by a sense of superiority. The Yankees have swagger and cockiness, each one of them. They *feel* superior. The Marines have and exhibit a spirit of "Gung Ho!" that is ridiculed yet envied by the other services. Johns Hopkins doctors, to put it bluntly, often are regarded as snobs in the world of medicine, because this is the implication of their general behavior. They are good and they know it. High morale cannot exist without a sense of superiority; it is thus inevitably akin to snobbishness.

Good morale, again as exemplified by these organizations, is self-sustaining and self-perpetuating. The Yankees have a history of victory that is perhaps more valuable than the stadium, the players, and the franchise. The Marines have more than a century of reputation as a tough, fighting outfit, to insure that the Corps will continue in that tradition. Johns Hopkins doctors have the memory of the "Big Four": Osler, Welch, Halsted, and Kelly, the exploits of Walter Reed and Jesse Lazear, of John Jacob Abel, Harvey Cushing, and Adolf Meyer, the repetition of challenging and difficult cases from all over the world, to sustain a continuance of that *élan* which is good morale. Once an organization has it, and the longer it has it, the easier it is to preserve and maintain.

2

Poor morale, on the other hand, suffers from *all* of the opposite attributes. It is always accompanied by a sense of inferiority; acquiescence to organization goals is indifferent and requires strong sanctions and rewards; and, worst of all, poor morale is not only self-perpetuating but also self-aggravating. An administrator can face no more difficult problem than that of transforming poor morale into good morale. This, in fact, is the crux of the matter. Analysis of the attributes of morale is well and good but administrators face the real problem: what to do about it.

Before attempting some general answers to this question and some examples of administrative action on morale, it should be made clear that I do not have much faith in such measurements of morale as are sometimes attempted. Labor turnover, lateness, absence, grievances, strikes can be quantified in various ways; indexes of these phenomena do tell something about morale in industrial and business organizations but they do not tell very much. Failures, drops, and withdrawals can be quantified too but they don't tell much about the morale of a student body. Percentages of men in the stockade, the number absent without leave, and the number of minor disciplinary infractions may be partial symptoms of military morale but they are not conclusive measures. Morale surveys can yield information of value, perhaps, but one never knows the extent to which answers are guided by the survey itself, or by the environment in which it is conducted. My thesis, then, is that the condition of morale must be felt rather than measured. I can offer no proofs of the arguments which follow.

3

Where organization morale is low, hope and anticipation of the future are likely to be dim. One requirement for raising morale is, somehow, the imparting of hope to the individuals who comprise the organization, to give them the uplifting idea that now, at last, the organization is "going somewhere."

Some years ago I saw this happen—unfortunately not for long—in a small company which I served for a time as consultant. This company would have been described as successful from its financial statements; it enjoyed a quasi-monopoly over a small segment of the market and had exploited that situation for many years, with substantial profits to absentee owners. During these lucrative years, technological development had been conspicuous by its absence and the organization itself had been going steadily down hill, in its volume of sales, in the opinions of its customers, and, most significantly, in the eyes of its own employees. These were for the most part a very long service group, as is usual in such cases. They were quite loyal but also quite dispirited. For too long the company had been "going nowhere," they would fill out their time and hope apathetically that the company would last long enough for this to happen.

Recognizing its firm financial position and technological potential, stock in the company was purchased by another organization, in sufficient amount to elect a new president and board chairman. I was retained by the new president and had some chance to observe his sensitivity to organization morale.

Closest to my own interest was his immediate adoption of two technological advances previously conceived within the company but allowed to lie dormant by his predecessor. This was less significant to over-all morale, perhaps, than other actions but, nevertheless, it had the effect of conveying to employees the general idea of revival, that the company now was on the march. The initiation of research directed toward more sweeping long-range developments was a step of the same kind.

To bolster the gradually sagging sales of company product, a defense contract was secured. This involved utilization of company facilities in a field of manufacturing foreign to the company's regular products but did have the short-run effect of providing security against short time and possible lay-offs. Again the morale effect was one of inducing hope, rather than lassitude or despair, for the future.

As might be expected in such an organization, wage levels were low, young blood was scarce, and long service and superannuated employees were numerous. The level of productivity corresponded to the level of wages; both were poor.

This kind of problem often has been attacked by the Duchess's policy of "off with his head!" Superannuated employees are told, with varying degrees of politeness or impoliteness, to get out. Those remaining are told to get on the ball or face the same treatment. And wages are raised only when the union has the strength to enforce its demands.

The new president showed more insight and imagination than this. He *wanted* to raise wages, not begrudgingly but as an act of policy, to revivify the work force and to make it possible for his personnel manager to hire new people in a tight labor market. He also wanted concurrently to raise productivity and he sought this on a cooperative, not a punitive, basis. When the union brought proposals for a new contract, with the usual demand for an across-the-board increase—albeit a modest one—he countered by proposing a *larger* increase, linked to an attainable rise in an over-all productivity index.

Bargaining sessions on this dramatic and extraordinary proposal proceeded from astonishment to suspicion to favorable consideration. Then, at the point of acceptance, the local union found it necessary to call in the attorney for the international union. I can only speculate that his general suspicion of *all* proposals advanced by management was deep-rooted; in any case, he killed the idea by flat refusal to give central office approval.

The venture, however, was by no means a total loss. Final settlement of the contract was amicable and not unfavorable to the company, and this certainly may be attributed in part to the evidence given by the company that it wanted to improve the employees' welfare. The attitudes of those on the negotiating committee of the local union gave support to this view.

Most of all, I think, the new president lifted morale by his treatment of the old-timers. There was no pension plan to provide for them, yet some of these senior people simply had to be replaced; they were no longer capable of doing their jobs well and could not possibly adapt to the changes that were under way. They could have been sacked, of course, but instead an attempt was made to find new uses for their accumulated experience. The factory manager was transferred from that active and demanding post to the task of developing improved engineering standards, a job he he could do well. The man who had conceived of the technological advances previously referred to was assigned to research, since he had ingenious ideas for further new developments. Comparable changes were made with other elderly members of the organization. All of these retentions cost money, which firing these people would have saved, but the net results, I am convinced, were in the company's favor in terms of morale.

This anecdote, unfortunately, does not have a happy ending. After the passage of a year or so, the new president resigned for reasons of his own and was replaced by another of quite different stripe. Heads began to roll and soon there was talk of a merger with another company in an altogether different field. A proxy fight and court action led finally to defeat of the merger but the morale damage, I'm sure, had been done. The aspirations and hopes raised by the first new president were killed by the punitive actions and threatened loss of company identification induced by the second.

As an aside pertinent to morale, this organization suffered from absentee ownership. Stock was held, by and large, by individuals, corporations, or estates, to whom only the regular, undiminished flow of dividends and market value of shares was important. No one at the top cared about the company as a living entity, no one at the top wore the old school tie. This was, and is always, a basic detriment to morale.

4

A much more dramatic example of morale improvement by the inducement of hope for the future can be cited from Bruce Catton's *A Stillness at Appomattox*[1], an eloquent narrative of the campaigns and battles of the Army of the Potomac from the time that Grant assumed over-all command until Lee surrendered at Appomatox. This was the army which had been beaten again and again by Lee until it had acquired a tradition, indeed, an expectation, of defeat. Grant, the new leader, was "the hammerer" who "at Fort Donelson and Vicksburg . . . had swallowed two

[1] New York, Doubleday & Co., Inc., 1953.

Confederate armies whole, and at Chattanooga . . . had driven a third army into headlong retreat."[2] But he had yet to tangle with the legendary Robert E. Lee.

On May 4, 1864, the Army of the Potomac crossed the Rapidan, as it had before, and on May 5 and 6 fought the bloody Battle of the Wilderness, emerging, as so often before, defeated. All day on May 7 the Union soldiers lay behind their breastworks waiting for the cover of darkness to permit withdrawal, and speculating that once more the Army would retreat across the Rapidan, to lick its wounds and prepare for the next futile campaign.

Instead, when the march began, the men found themselves on the Brock Road headed south. ". . . The road was crowded, and nobody could see much, but as the men trudged along it suddenly came to them that this march was different. Just then there was a crowding at the edge of the road, and mounted aides were ordering: 'Give way to the right.' and a little cavalcade came riding by at an easy jingling trot—and there, just recognizable, was Grant riding in the lead, his staff following him, heading south.

"This army had known dramatic moments of inspiration in the past—massed flags and many bugles and broad blue ranks spread out in the sunlight, with leadership bearing a drawn sword and riding a prancing horse, and it had been grand and stirring. Now there was nothing more than a bent shadow in the night, a stoop-shouldered man who was saying nothing to anyone, methodically making his way to the head of the column—and all of a moment the tired column came alive, and a wild cheer broke the night and men tossed their caps in the darkness.

"They had had their fill of desperate fighting, and this pitiless little man was leading them into nothing except

[2] Ibid., p. 40.

more fighting, and probably there would be no end to it, but at least he was not leading them back in sullen acceptance of defeat, and somewhere, many miles ahead, there would be victory for those who lived to see it. So there was tremendous cheering, and Grant's big horse Cincinnati caught the excitement and reared and pranced, and as he got him under control Grant told his staff to have the men stop cheering because the Rebels were not far away and they would hear and know that a movement was being made.

"It was the same on other roads. Sedgwick's men backtracked to Chancellorsville, and as the men reached that fatal crossroads the veterans knew that if they took the left-hand fork they would be retreating and if they turned to the right they would be going on for another fight. The column turned right, and men who made the march wrote that with that turn there was a quiet relaxing of the tension and a lifting of gloom, so that men who had been slogging along quietly began to chatter as they marched. Here and there a regiment sang a little."[3]

5

In both of these examples improved morale came about from arousing hope for the future, rather than from any change in material welfare. This is a point which merits clinching.

In fancy, imagine two different organizations, one of which brings to its members a total quantity of satisfactions S. Let it be assumed that the second organization provides several times as many satisfactions to its members as the first, represented, say, by $4S$. Under such conditions,

[3] Ibid., pp. 91, 92. Quoted by permission of Doubleday and Company, Inc.

the morale of the second organization is likely to be higher than that of the first. While this is not necessarily so, assume that it is for the moment.

Now let it be assumed that by some means the members of the first, low morale outfit are caused to believe that tomorrow will be better. Under such conditions, even though the aggregate satisfactions of the two organizations remain in ratio one to four, the morale of the first organization will rise and can quite easily come to exceed that of its more opulent neighbor. It is the promise and hope for change for the better which counts, not the static, absolute situation.

The current state of affairs in Soviet Russia and the United States is, possibly, exemplary of just this sort of thing. Our own material welfare—and our spiritual welfare too—has been far greater than that ever enjoyed by the citizens of Russia. We often use this fact to comfort ourselves that the dictatorial Soviet regime cannot last, because it does not bring adequate benefactions to its citizens. But this rationale can miss the point: if enough Russians believe that tomorrow will be better, then their national spirit, their morale, can very well come to exceed our own. It is not necessary that any particular tomorrow *be* better but only that this be the current, live hope.

Disillusionment through failure to realize such hopes may some day change Russian morale for the worse but that does not appear to be the case just now. That they aspire to better things is the important point.

6

Grant's dramatic action after the Battle of the Wilderness had given hope for the future to the dispirited Army of the

Potomac and had thereby raised its morale. But the narrative tells more than this. Hope and aspiration are important ingredients of improved morale and so also are common suffering and the common conquest of obstacles.

It would be folly to suggest that an administrator expose his organization to suffering on the scale of war in order to improve morale but the relationship between common suffering and morale is no less real on this account. Adolf Hitler, in fact, did something very like this in the 1930's, with salutary effect upon German morale. Despite Hitler, this kind of action *is* feasible in appropriate degree.

Consider the Massachusetts Institute of Technology, for example, where students hang pennant-slogans in their rooms saying "Tech is Hell." Is this a criticism or complaint about their alma mater, a symptom of poor morale? Of course not. Paradoxical or not, it is a badge of honor, a notice that the students belong to a select group, a symptom of very high morale deriving from common suffering under rigorous curricula.

Industry and business are replete with examples—and with opportunities—of the same kind. Enlist the aid of a group of employees in meeting some extraordinary deadline. To succeed they must "suffer" together in some way, by working longer, or harder, or missing a social engagement, or going without dinner. Does the sacrifice impair morale? By no means; it has the opposite effect.

Eleemosynary and social organizations are very conscious of this fact. Skilled administrators always see to it that the church has a mortgage, the hospital a debt, the university a deficit, which organization members must strive to overcome. Athletics, military service, school, church, all partake of this same characteristic. Common suffering—it is better to say common sacrifice on common enterprises—

welds organizations together and lifts morale. This is a principle administrators *can* act upon.

They must, however, do so with care. Common sacrifice on common enterprises requires success, not failure, if morale is to be improved. Obstacles must be *over*come, not *under*come—if I may coin a word—to result in improved morale.

Let the industrial administrator ask his people to strive for a deadline which *can* be met and success will raise morale. Let him set a too difficult or unattainable goal and failure will harm the very thing he seeks to help. Let the church mortgage be paid off and ceremoniously burned and the morale of the congregation will rise—but not if the bank forecloses. Let the football coach condition his men by hard, demanding effort and their morale will be lifted by common sacrifice and self-discipline—but the coach had better schedule a few potential victories.

Morale can be raised, then, by taking administrative advantage of common sacrifice, accompanied by common victories over obstacles. However, this is by no means as easy as it sounds, because the obstacles to be overcome must be attainable and, at the same time, difficult. There is no morale merit in meeting a deadline that is merely routine, nor any in burning a piddling mortgage, nor any in beating teams that are known to be pushovers. Only tough, yet attainable goals will do and they are neither easy for an administrator to come by or to risk, once they are at hand.

7

The environment of administration, however, is ever-changing and dynamic, and administrators will find obstacles and opportunities made for them, simply by the passage of time. If they are alert they may consciously utilize events for morale purposes. Opportunities of this kind already have been described in other contexts—the keyboard case (pp. 5–27), the Rollins case (pp. 127–134)—and one more will be given here to sharpen the point.

Twelve O'Clock High, by Beirne Lay, Jr. and Sy Bartlett[4] is, in a sense, an entire novel devoted to the problem of raising morale in the 918th "Hard Luck Group" of the Eighth Air Force in World War II. The central figure of the story is Brigadier-General Frank Savage, who was assigned to command the group for the specific purpose of reviving its flagging spirit and low morale. He did so by a series of dramatic and self-sacrificing actions which make good reading and reveal keen insight on the part of the authors. Only one of these actions need be presented here to illustrate what I have called the conscious utilization of events for morale purposes.

Five groups of bombers, outward bound across the Channel, were forced down to 4000 feet under heavy cloud cover. Because of this, headquarters transmitted the recall order and four of the groups turned back. Savage, leading the 918th, feigned not to hear—he later broke a radio tube with his gloved hand to support his excuse—and continued to lead the 918th toward the enemy coast. The clouds lifted, he took his group to 21,000 feet, bombed the railway marshalling yards at Liège, and brought them all safely home.

This is the kind of luck only found in novels, to be sure, but the point is there. By utilizing the opportunity to induce a sense of superiority in his hitherto inferior group Frank Savage did more to raise morale than a thousand

[4] New York, Harper Brothers, 1948.

eloquent pep-talks could have accomplished. The 918th did something done by no other group, this made them better and they knew it.

8

No discussion of administrative measures for raising morale would be complete without correlative mention of participation as an essential ingredient. This already has been done, in a sense, by emphasizing *common* suffering, *common* sacrifice, and *common* victories over obstacles. Participation, however, means more than this, in the manner of the Hawthorn Experiments and the stipulations made elsewhere in these pages (p. 81). For morale to rise, when it is at low ebb, it is important that the rank and file participate, insofar as it is feasible for them to do so, in decisions affecting their own welfare. I have seen such a transformation take place by the formation and action of an industrial employee committee but the Hawthorn Experiments themselves are a far better example. "Management and the Worker"[5] will reward the reader on this point.

9

This discussion so far has assumed that it is a good thing for an administrator to act toward the improvement of morale in the organization or segment of organization that he directs. When he utilizes events as Frank Savage did, puts his people to the test, turns south upon the Wilderness Road, proposes a wage increase beyond the union's demand, the administrator achieves a net gain but he does not do so without cost.

The slogan "Tech is Hell" is a banner of victory for those

[5] F. J. Roethlisberger and W. J. Dickson, *Management and the Worker*. Cambridge, Harvard University Press, 1940.

who graduate but it can be so only because of those who fail, and it is certainly no banner to them. Superiority is a relative thing and when it relates to human rather than physical entities, it is necessary for some to feel inferior in order that others feel superior. This is by no means an unmixed blessing.

Raising morale by the sacrifice-obstacle method involves risks, as I have said. Incurring these is costly to the administrator himself, as in the case of General Savage, whose nerves finally gave way under the strains of risks for morale purposes. This is part of the strain of administration in every kind of organization and it is a real strain indeed.

Despite this negative attribute, I am virtuously in favor of high morale and would like to have the administrative adroitness to raise it to the very top in the organization under my direction. Morale is good, perhaps good enough, but I would prefer, as one colleague put the matter quite seriously, to make ours "the best School of Engineering in the world." This implies many criteria of excellence, with morale a most important factor.

How to do this? I do not really know.

I can define morale after a fashion and sense its characteristics. I can discuss and exemplify administrative actions directed toward the induction of hope and aspiration, the utilization of events, the values of common sacrifice and common victory, the enlistment of participation. But when I am asked point blank how to raise morale where it is my responsibility to do so, I must, to be honest, confess that I do not know.

This does not mean that I am not trying or that I will not continue to try. It does mean that the art of criticism is easier than the art of successful administration.

XIV

On Communication—I

COMPRISING, as it does, the major part of all human intercourse, communication is a vast field and one of great significance to all administrators, who, perforce, must communicate with their subordinates, peers, and superiors, and in turn receive communication from them, if organizations are to function.

Communication of one kind or another, no doubt, has existed since life on earth began, but only recently has the subject itself been exposed to intensive analysis and investigation. The study of language, through linguistics and semantics, has gone beyond grammar, vocabulary, and rhetoric, to explore the effect of language itself upon the formulation of our thoughts, the development of individual, national, and racial psychologies, and the effect of words and other forms of communication upon our emotions. Symbolic logic has emerged from the more general field of philosophy with an algebra of its own with which to deal with problems of communication. Communication theory has brought concepts of "bits" of information and "noise" which permit mathematical exploration, something called "information theory" has evolved, the role of redundancy has been investigated, communication networks have been subjected to controlled experiment, the concept of entropy has been applied to messages, and a new word, *cybernetics*, has been coined by Professor Wiener to describe his own researches in communication.[1]

All this sounds more lofty and sophisticated than is intended, as though I know all about these things and could write about them with intelligence and penetration. On the contrary, they have been cited because I do *not* know about them and have neither the knowledge nor the temerity to discuss communication in any but a pragmatic way.

2

Administrators, as I have already said, must send and receive communications if their organizations are to function. In recent years, as organizations have become what might be called more democratic and persuasion has had to replace fiat, administrators have been urged and entreated from all sides to Communicate with a capital C. Workers, it is said, will be happier, more loyal, more productive, more stable, more tractable, if they are kept informed about the organization, its health or sickness, its

---

[1] Perhaps a personal comment may be forgiven. Being incapable of comprehending it, I have not read Professor Wiener's *Cybernetics* (Cambridge, Mass., Massachusetts Institute of Technology Press, 1948) but did read his *Human Use of Human Beings* (Boston, Houghton Mifflin Co., 1950), which purported to be a presentation of the subject understandable to a layman. This experience gave me the feeling that cybernetics is much less a new field of scholarship than a clever and euphonious new word. Having coined a new word, one is beguiled into believing that something new must be described by it.

I had the same feeling when, in World War II, Winston Churchill urged invasion of "the soft underbelly of Europe." His frequent urging of this finally convinced me that he was persuaded more by his own eloquence than by the feasibility of such a strategy. Having characterized the Mediterranean coast as a "soft underbelly," it had to be that way, easily penetrable by the "spearhead" of an expeditionary force. Conversely, such a "spearhead" would be "blunted" by the impenetrability of "Fortress Europe" along the English Channel.

All of us, I am sure, fall into this trap from time to time.

policies, its progress, its intentions, etc., etc., etc. Communication, we are also told, is a two-way street; there must be upward, as well as downward, communication, and much is made of the cathartic effect of allowing the rank and file to get things off their collective and individual chests. Thus, communication has become an administrative virtue as well as a necessity.

Partly because of this, I suppose, a wide variety of communicative devices, unheard of a quarter century or more ago, have appeared on the scene. Employee-management committees and works councils have been born and have proliferated in industry, in order that management and rank and file may confer face to face. House magazines, which used to be slanted toward customers as institutional advertising, now are directed toward the organization's own family and have become as folksy, with names and pictures, as the old-fashioned country newspaper. Once dry-as-dust corporate reports have been jazzed up with colors, pie charts, bar charts, non-technical language, and photographs, and given wide circulation beyond the customary stockholder mailing list. Public address systems have become only less familiar than the telephone; these give executives the added capability of informing and/or exhorting all of their fellows simply by pressing the switch of the "squawk box" and talking into its microphone.

This is stated with some sarcasm and perhaps a touch of cynicism, which may suggest a belief that communication is not a virtue, that labor-management committees are administratively bad, house organs a form of insincere propaganda, and so on. The intent is not to suggest this but only to lead into a discussion of three fallacies:

　1. That administrative communication need consist only of *telling*.

2. That administrative communication need consist only of *listening*.

3. That communication of decisions to subordinates before taking action upon them equates to sharing authority for the decisions themselves.

Admittedly, these are overstated and oversimplified; administrators would disavow all of them, the first and second as untrue and contradictory, and the third as fact and not fallacy. No administrator would admit to a belief in communication as only an act of informing (i.e., telling) subordinates, yet many behave as if this were so. Not so many similarly rely upon listening in a kind of exclusive sense but some have. The belief that communication of decision in advance of action and sharing of authority are inseparable is almost universal.

3

Several years ago I was retained by a small manufacturing company to give a series of lectures on management topics to their supervisory group. A few months afterward, I was invited to be an observer at an "Employee-Management Committee" meeting. This committee had been formed by the president of the company, in the belief that regular meetings of such a body would improve relations between employees and management and enhance morale.

The meeting lasted about an hour in an atmosphere that was, outwardly at least, quite agreeable. The demeanor of the president and his management cohorts was warm and friendly enough but, even so, the four or five employee representatives present uttered not one word until the last few minutes of the meeting. They were told about inventory problems in the store room and tool room, about the seriousness of current spoilage, and about sales and production prospects of the company. These involved expositions by several management participants, and some discourse between them, but no employee said anything whatever about these topics. Finally, one of the employees did speak, to ask if any decision had been made upon a request, apparently tendered at a previous meeting, that paid vacations be granted for the four week-days following Labor Day. The reply to this inquiry was brief: he was told by the president, in a tone clearly implying negation, that the management was "thinking about it." Just after this the meeting was adjourned.

Such descriptions of situations, in which the bosses do all the talking is so familiar as to be hackneyed. Yet that is precisely why it is important. It describes administrative behavior that is typical and familiar. Again and again and again, the boss *tells* the employees what *he* wants them to know, or what *he* thinks they ought to know. What *they* want to know is not a consideration.

The fact that this is typical and familiar does not make it wrong, of course. It is fair to ask which is better: informing employees about inventory problems, spoilage, and production prospects, or telling them nothing at all? As communication is currently revered as good for its own sake, one would be inclined to say that *any* information is better than *no* information. By forming the committee and telling the employees about various matters, the management may not have communicated in the best way but they have at least done something of value.

But this is not necessarily so, not by any means. Previously, when there was no Employee-Management Committee, employees were not told about the things their representatives now learned. But previously the employees had not *expected* to be told. When a committee is formed, expectation is aroused; the employees expect not only to be told but themselves to do a bit of telling. If this expectation is only half fulfilled, disillusionment is likely to be severe and may cost more than the gain. Thus, introduction of one-way communication where formerly there was none can result in net loss rather than net gain.

In any event, the tendency for superiors to do most of the talking is both natural and understandable. Without implying an exclusive monologue by the superior, he will be more likely to communicate *to* the subordinate than vice versa because:

1. He will have more to say. He will know more about the enterprise than the subordinate and he is habituated to communicating to him by the usual needs of giving orders, instructions, and information. Ordinarily there is more to be communicated downward than upward in any organizational hierarchy. Administrators possess more information than subordinates, are accustomed to imparting it, and the custom itself will tend to inhibit upward communication to some degree.

2. The superior is a human being and prefers to talk rather than to listen. The subordinate is a human being too and has the same preference, but he is not in the same dominant position—except to *his* subordinates—to exercise it.

3. The superior will be much, much less restrained in the content, nature, and tone of his communications than his subordinates. They, the subordinates, inevitably are dependent to some degree upon the superior for the satisfaction of their wants and, because of this, will temper every communication to the boss, whether by spoken word, written word, gesture, or demeanor, to avoid giving

offense. Only in the heat of anger or provocation, or when protected by something like a labor union, will the subordinate cast this precaution aside.

4

This third reason for executive dominance of communication, for emphasis upon "telling," merits further examination. Consider the Employee-Management Committee meeting and the final, timidly presented question about paid vacations after Labor Day. Superficially, this request seems to contain nothing critical of management; it asks for four days of holiday. This would stop production and cost money, the firm cannot afford the extra cost, therefore the request is denied. All of this is completely temperate, completely objective, completely logical. There is really nothing for management to get hurt or huffy about; there is really nothing for the employees to be timid or restrained about.

Not so. The request for four days' holiday involves production and dollars, to be sure, but more than that, it is also an expression of discontent. And, if the employees are discontented, then the management is at fault. Management has been something less than perfect in administering the firm's affairs; otherwise there would be no complaint.

This is the subtle but inevitable implication of the request; this is why it is hesitantly and timidly made, brusquely and evasively answered—even though neither the employee nor his boss understood or consciously considered their own behavior. This is the inescapable implication of *any* subordinate complaint or demand, in *any* form of organization. Subordinates will stifle some complaints and some demands just to avoid being stigmatized as chronic complainers but this is a minor blockade to upward communication compared to the obstacles of implied criticism. We scorn and derogate a "yes man" because he says only what he thinks his boss will want to hear. We admire a "no man" for having the courage to speak his own mind. But all of us, every one, are yes men and no men to some degree. We are all governed by the same subtle forces that restrained the employee representative and antagonized his superior.

5

Within a year or so after the meeting just described, the company was organized by a labor union and there was a six-week strike before agreement was reached on the first contract. This was followed by the usual spate of grievances, some of them going all the way to arbitration for settlement.

These expressions of discontent were critical of management too, not subtly like the request for post-Labor Day vacation, but militantly, harshly, and openly, with hostility rather than timidity. Now the employees had no fear of management reprisals; they had their union behind them. The restraints to critical upward communication had been removed.

Burleigh B. Gardner and Charles R. Moore, in "Human Relations in Industry,"[2] have commented upon this apropos of the unique organization roles of labor unions with respect to upward communication. In a very real sense each union is a part of the organization of each establishment under contract. Yet the union stands outside the parent organization, independent of its authority but

[2] Chicago, Richard D. Irwin, Inc., 1950.

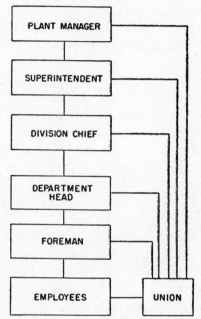

Fig. 8. Organization relationship of a labor union.

with communication access to every level of the hierarchy, without fear of management reprisal (Fig. 8).

The removal of these customary restraints can give management a very hard time. Management wants upward communication and, with a union, gets it with a vengeance. Subordinates are now free to criticize and complain without fear of punishment. And they are also free to give vent to their pent-up frustrations, to rebel against authority, to "spit in the boss's eye," to "singe the management's tail."[3] It is much easier for an administrator to agree

[3] This is a somewhat bowdlerized version of a statement made frequently by the local president of a shipyard union. He usually preceded the statement by saying that he liked nothing better.

philosophically that upward communication is desirable than it is for him to cope with it in reality.

This raises a very difficult question: if free and candid communication up as well as down the organization hierarchy is desirable, should administrators encourage the removal of restraints that inhibit criticism?

It is easy for me, a university professor and dean, to answer this affirmatively, because I am not on the labor-management firing line and can be detached about the whole thing. How, it is more to the point to ask, would I feel about a union of students who could criticize teachers without the restraints they now feel? How would I feel if they spit in *my* eye, singed *my* tail?

Like the industrial manager, I would not like it but I hope that I would regard such a development as a good thing for the organization to which I am attached. Indeed, I will go further and argue that students often need something like a union, not for purposes of collective bargaining, but for the encouragement of candid and critical communication to their superiors.

The relationship between a good teacher and his students is probably the very best element in all of education, but not all teachers can be classed as good. Some are incompetent, incapable of teaching, and some are tyrants, who find the classroom about as convenient as a drill field or even a prison for the exercise of their dictatorial tendencies. The teacher, any teacher who wants to, can rub his pupils' noses in the dirt—and some do.

Like everyone else, I had as a student, both good and bad teachers, and revered the good ones and endured the bad, never having had sufficient provocation to run the risk of complaining about the incompetents or rebelling against the tyrants. But sometimes I would have liked to rebel and believe that it would have been good for me and good for the institutions I attended if ready means for critical communication of and to my superiors had been provided.

However, I do not espouse the development of such extra-organization attachments lightly or unreservedly, for they sound better than they really are. For one thing—and many would consider this the strongest objection—they are somewhat destructive of executive authority. Certainly labor unions have sharply curtailed administrative power in business and industry, detrimentally some will say. Certainly we would all feel misgivings about militant unions of students, which might bring forth desirable upward communication but also bring anarchy to the classroom. Certainly we would shrink from the notion of a union of rank and file soldiers, who might thus be motivated to refuse the orders of their officers at a critical time.

These objections from the standpoint of those in administration can be supported by comparable objections from the standpoint of the individual.

The industrial labor union and its members do have unrestrained communication access to any level of the parent organization and do not fear executive reprisal. But the union itself is not a box on the table of organization, like that shown in Fig. 8, it is a hierarchy more like that shown in Fig. 9. By belonging to the union, the individual employee has been relieved of fear and restraint in communicating with his employers and superiors but, by the same token, he has acquired a whole new set of superiors and, with them, a whole new set of restraints. Now he can spit in his company boss's eye but, mayhap, not even dare to look into his union boss's eye. What coal

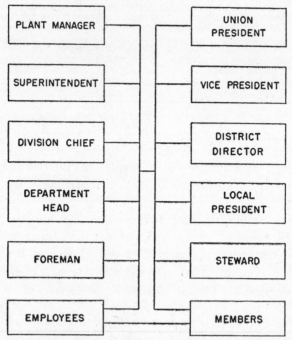

FIG. 9. Organization relationship of a labor union, including the union hierarchy.

miner, to choose an obvious example, would recklessly criticize John L. Lewis? Who knows? Perhaps we shall some day have unions within unions just on this account.

6

Preceding pages have rambled a good deal about the general fallacy of communication à la telling, by exploring the forces conducive to executive dominance of communication and the counter forces that are released when restraints to upward communication are removed. These counter forces become apparent only when organization by something like a labor union releases them, or under conditions of sufficient provocation where there is no union. For the most part, since most of the very many different kinds of organization are not unionized and provocative crises are exceptional, the executive continues to dominate communication and to *tell* his subordinates what *he* wants them to know.

If this is to be improved upon, without the creation of an outside organization akin to a union, the administrator must become conscious of the restraints upon his subordinates and by his own conduct seek to relieve or to ameliorate them. If he *wants* his subordinates' ideas, suggestions, complaints, and criticisms, he must suppress his desire to talk and school himself to listen. He must become aware that complaints connote criticism of him as an administrator. For his natural inclination to be hurt and antagonistic from these implied or stated criticisms he must substitute the responsiveness which has been defined and emphasized repeatedly throughout these pages.

If his organization has a union or the like attached to it, he may rightly resist encroachment upon his authority but this does not mean that he cannot seek to utilize the valuable communication channels now provided for him. And finally, if he is devoted to the welfare of the individuals under his direction, he will be conscious that their union, or whatever the extra-organization may be, can impose just as many restraints as he once could himself. He may not be able to alter such a situation but, being perceptive, he may oppose it and perhaps exert desirable influence on behalf of his own people.

XV

On Communication—II

AT the opposite pole to communication by telling is communication by listening. Obviously, telling can never wholly exclude listening and vice versa. The boss who is said to do "all the talking" will not conduct a monologue but will do some listening. Even the psychoanalyst who encourages his patient on the couch to talk will himself do some talking to his patient. Whether telling or listening dominates in communication is a question of degree and emphasis.

In at least one quite significant instance a large corporation sought to reverse the usual emphasis upon telling in favor of a very strong emphasis upon listening. The corporation, the American Telephone and Telegraph Company, did this without the compulsion of a labor union, deliberately and voluntarily, as a consequence of research done at the plant of a subsidiary, the Hawthorne plant of the Western Electric Company in Chicago.[1]

At Hawthorne two investigations of the effect of working conditions upon productivity were undertaken in 1927, jointly by a group from within the company and from the Graduate School of Business Administration of Harvard University. In a room devoted to the wiring of telephone

---

[1] See F. J. Roethlisberger and William J. Dickson, *Management and the Worker*, Cambridge, Harvard University Press, 1940; North Whitehead, *The Industrial Worker*, Cambridge, Harvard University Press, 1938; and Elton Mayo, *The Human Problems of an Industrial Civilization*, Cambridge, Harvard University Press, 1933.

banks by wiremen, soldermen, and inspectors on group piece-work, an observer remained for many months studying the "informal organization" among the rank and file, the social forces at work within the group. By this means he came to perceive that the wage incentive did not motivate as it was supposed to. Instead of seeking to earn more by producing more, output was very carefully controlled by the operators themselves at a level which they, rather than the industrial engineers or management, had set. Strong sanctions were imposed by the group upon the "chiselers" who produced below the group norm and upon the "rate busters" who produced above—even though these faster workers increased the wages of their fellows.

In another room, devoted to the assembly of relays by girls also on group piece-work, meticulous measurements of output were kept during control periods and again after changes had been made in lighting, working hours, rest periods, and the like. Large increases in output were achieved and it was believed that these gains derived from the improved working conditions. The final step, however, disproved this belief: working conditions which had prevailed at the outset were restored but output remained at the experimental high level.

Thus the researchers were confounded by each investigation. Results of study in the bank-wiring room disproved, or at the very least tended to disprove, that wage incentives motivate as is commonly believed. Studies of the relay-assembly room at first indicated that productivity is dependent upon favorable working conditions and then seemed to disprove this because high output was sustained when original, less favorable conditions were restored.

Since the relay-assembly girls were on the same kind of

group piece-work as the bank-wiring men, and had been before assignment to the test-room, it could be reasoned that the increased production of relays was not due to motivation from the wage incentive. Since it was not due, either, to the various improvements in environment, to what was it due?

Reexamination of the entire experimental procedure led to the conclusion that the carefully controlled experiments had not been controlled at all. Lighting in Period A could be changed to different and presumably better lighting in Period B; the difference in lighting could be measured and related to measured differences in output between the periods, while all other variables were held constant. Then improved production could be related directly to improved lighting. This was the reasoning.

But all other variables were *not* held constant. The most important variable of all, the emotions of the operators, could neither be controlled nor measured.

Realization of this finally led to the conclusion that it was the changes themselves, not their physical nature but the *facts* of change, and how the changes were introduced, that had raised production, and had kept it high when the old conditions were restored.

To take a girl out of a huge relay-assembly department and invite her into a test-room is to notice her and her test-room companions. To ask for opinions about a rest-period before introducing such a change is to invite participation in decisions close to the operators' working lives. To do this repeatedly, while a research observer becomes a friend and confidant and at the same time is not a boss, is to raise production. This is what had happened.

Much of this was a matter of communication—upward communication. The girls were *asked* if they would go into the test-room, *asked* if they would be willing to work under brighter lights, *asked* if they would try a ten-minute rest period each morning and afternoon, *asked* if they would go back to the old, less pleasant conditions at the very end.

The asking, moreover, was quite different from the kind portrayed in the cartoon, where the boss eyes his employees balefully and says, "Any comments from those who expect to resign?" No doubt the girls were influenced in some degree by the usual superior-subordinate restraints, no doubt they sometimes acquiesced because they thought they were expected to, but these tendencies were offset by the research itself, by the fact that their opinions were elicited by investigators rather than bosses, and by continued responsiveness to what the girls said.

Thus the results achieved were in substantial measure due to enhanced upward communication.

2

As a consequence of this and also because of other, related experiences, a vast upward communications program evolved and spread into many A.T.&T. units throughout the country. The basis of this program was the employee interview, not the kind of interview which takes place in the employment office, nor like that between a worker and his boss, but a special kind of interview with a special kind of interviewer, trained carefully in the techniques of eliciting the employee's thoughts, in getting him to "open up," to "get things off his chest."

More specifically, training was given to a considerable number of "industrial relations counselors," whose missions were to interview the employees who volunteered for their services. It was understood that all disclosures would be kept in strict confidence; if an employee reviled his boss—or for that matter his wife—his revulsion was not disclosed to management or to anyone else. If all of the employees from a given department, independently but unanimously reviled the boss they shared in common, this too would be kept secret and presumably the detested and reviled executive would stay at his post.

Thus the therapy, somewhat like psychoanalysis and the Roman Catholic confessional, was intended to be catharsis. In effect, management said, we will not devote ourselves to giving information to our employees, we will elicit it from them. To do this, we must establish conditions of confidence favorable to freedom of expression and candor, and this requires that we learn nothing of what the employees disclose and take no action upon such complaints as they may voice. By this means, however, we shall relieve the pent-up frustrations of our workers and thereby improve motivation, morale, and production.

There followed a vast listening campaign. In one plant, if memory serves correctly, some 40,000 interviews were conducted, some of them of two hours' duration and some repeated with the same employees, as might be expected. Some successes were reported. One employee, for example, complained about the food in the cafeteria and then, in the next interview, expressed gratification over the improvement, although nothing had been done. There were other instances of the same kind and, for a time, enthusiasm for the counseling program was high.

As in the case of the Employee-Management Committee, it is fair to ask if this program of listening was not better than no upward communication at all. Undoubtedly many of the interviews did yield beneficial catharsis and did raise the morale and loyalty of some employees. But, again, there must have been many, many others who wanted more than catharsis, who wanted to see their complaints and frustrations acted upon, whose frustrations must have been aggravated rather than relieved by the confidential, do-nothing policy. Entirely apart from the very considerable cost of interviewing, it is quite possible that the program resulted in a net loss. In any case, whether because of high out-of-pocket cost or inadequate results, the program has virtually been abandoned. Optimum communication is more than telling—and also more than listening.

In fairness to the researchers and to the sponsoring corporation, no one else quite knows what to do about the Hawthorne results either, although their significance is widely acknowledged. Some executives, as I have already said, have latched on to communication as a cure-all virtue and some have gone in for employee "participation" and something called "human relations" as a kind of gimmick to keep workers happy and raise production. Any such approach misses the essence of the relay-assembly room research.

The Hawthorne experiments did not set out to manipulate people into being happy or to do more work, either by talking to them or by listening to them, or by tossing them a bone of token participation. Both the communication and the participation were genuine and sincere, without ulterior motive; there was an essential "togetherness" about the whole thing. When organizations and the administrators who lead them are capable of achieving that spirit, then the results of the relay-assembly room may be duplicated. Until then, as long as communication is told only to guide or direct, or heard only as catharsis; as long as participation is invited only to motivate, the potential of the experiments will not be realized.

3

To examine the third fallacy, that communication of decision prior to execution equates to sharing of authority, it is necessary first to establish certain conditions.

First, there is no conflict between what has previously been said about participation and this discussion about advance communication and the sharing of authority. Participation and sharing authority are parts of the same thing, to be sure; one cannot have participation without giving a share in decision making. But this does not say that *communication* of decision in advance of action is to share the power to decide. That is what so many believe, or at least behave as though they do.

With this in mind, suppose that the administrator of an organization—any organization, or any segment of an organization—decides upon a course of action known to be esteemed or desired by all. In such cases, announcement of intention is likely to be in advance of action and involves no challenge of authority, since there is little possibility of conflict. If an army officer decides to give extra leave to his men, he does not hesitate to give them the welcome news in advance. If an industrial or business executive decides to redecorate the cafeteria or locker rooms, he is likely to announce his intentions to his employees, in fair certainty that they will be pleased. If a teacher decides to cancel a previously announced examination, he can be reasonably sure that his students will not dispute his decision. No question of rank and file or subordinate challenge to authority is involved in the advance communication of glad tidings.

This is not true when the news is bad. Let the officer cancel leaves which previously have been granted and the response from his men will be quite different. Let the executive decide to eliminate an existing cafeteria in order to cut down monetary loss and the response of the rank and file will be anything but jubilant. Without warning, let the teacher spring a quiz on his students; they may not openly rebel, but their displeasure will be clearly apparent and they may in some degree challenge the teacher's authority to give the unannounced examination.

Between the better and the bitter kinds of decisions which must be communicated there are blends of each. The better kinds do not arouse resistance or objection, the bitter kinds do. In the latter case, how shall this resistance be met? What kind of communication, transmitted when, will effect the best transition?

Again, we may discuss extremes. At one extreme, communication may be postponed until the moment of action: the soldier is packed and ready to go when his leave is canceled, the employees learn of discontinuance of cafeteria service when dismantling begins, the students find out about the quiz when it is handed to them. At the opposite extreme, the same decisions are made but are promptly communicated, not deferred. What is the relative net economy of these different approaches?

From the administrative standpoint the moment of action kind of announcement has certain attractions. It permits postponement of both bad tidings and conflict and gives the executive a chance to indulge in procrastination, a temptation very dear to everyone. Moreover, this kind of action seems to preserve both speed and authority. The executive makes his own decision and proceeds to carry it out, there is no delay for communication or for argument. Communication, when it comes, is of a *fait accompli* kind; the rank and file may protest, even violently, but their protest will be at the *nature* of the action and not at the *right* of the administrator to decide as he did.

However, deferred communication has negative attributes as well. Expressions like, "You could at least have let me know," "Why didn't you tell me?" and "You might have given me a little notice," are heard frequently in and out of organization life and are indicative of the resentments we all feel upon getting last-minute information. I do not think I have ever heard deferred communication described as discourteous but there is in such situations a failure to consider the feelings of others, an element of incivility, which probably accounts for much of the resentment aroused.

Resentment also has more practical causes. Subordinates tend to suspect the motives of their superiors' decisions and failure to communicate the reasons for intended action often results in misunderstanding. Advance communication at least offers the possibility of making clear the reasons for decision and prevents erroneous and damaging assumptions.

Then, too, people tend to make plans of one kind or another and these are more likely to be disrupted by last-minute news than by earlier information, which may give time for change and adjustment. I have seen employees disgruntled even at good news on this account: "If I had only known about this holiday in advance, I would have planned a trip to the sea-shore."

Deferred communication also loses for the administrator the chance of receiving and responding to improvements in the decisions he has made. A decision to eliminate a money-losing cafeteria may be quite sound but that does not preclude the possibility that some rank and file employee can suggest a better way to retain some measure of food service without monetary loss. Such ideas have much more value than their own merit; they involve chances for executive responsiveness, employee participation, identification with the enterprise, enhancement of communications per se, and contribute largely to morale.

This is a negative value of deferred communication and, correspondingly, a positive value of advance communication. In each case, whatever the news to be imparted, this value can and often does exceed all of the others. It alone can tilt the scales in favor of communication of decision in advance of action.

4

If advance communication is so much better, why do we not have more of it?

Two reasons on behalf of administrators have been given: (1) human tendencies to postpone unpleasantness, to procrastinate, and (2) desire to preserve executive authority. But the second of these reasons is not one-sided; the executive acts to preserve authority because he knows that his subordinates will use the information, if he communicates it in advance of action, to challenge his right to make the decision itself. If this is so, as I think it is, and if the lower echelons of organization want advance communication, as I think they do, then they, the lower echelons, must come to understand that advance communications give information and do not, of necessity ask permission.

Failure to understand this distinction is perhaps most evident in union-management relations, not in collective bargaining, but during the life of a collective agreement. Let management make a decision legally theirs under the contract, let them state their intentions in advance to the union, and the response is likely to be an attempt to block the decision itself. This is understandable enough but it does militate against future communication in advance of action.

An example of this kind of challenging union behavior was witnessed at another arbitration hearing between the company and union involved in the Rollins case (Chapter XII). In this case, the company decided to transfer certain mechanical department employees across craft lines to meet a temporary production need. Subject to the requirement that they maintain craft distinction "whenever possible," the contract gave permission for such a transfer.

As part of a policy of communicating decisions in advance of action, two union stewards were informed of the intended transfer; they in turn reported to their union officers and an attempt was made to block the move, culminating finally in a grievance carried to arbitration. In view of the qualifying clause pledging observance of craft lines "whenever possible," the dispute was legitimate enough and the incident is not told just because the union tried to block the action.

What was revealing, apropos of advance communication, was the testimony of one union man who accused the company of being remiss in discussing the transfer with the stewards and asked, "Why were the stewards told about the intended transfer, if not to ask their permission?" To this man—and, one may surmise, to his colleagues too—a statement of decision, e.g., "We intend. . . ," at once translates into a request for permission: "May we . . . ?" This is precisely the fallacy which has been discussed through these many pages: that communication of decision in advance of action and execution equates to sharing authority, to asking permission. It does not, or, more realistically, should not, for optimum communication in any organization.

XVI

On Executive and Organization Overload

BEGINNING approximately in 1940 the tempo of business and industry in the United States, and elsewhere in the world too, quickened because of war. It was only two years later, after Pearl Harbor, that President Roosevelt proclaimed the 48-hour week; factories which had been on one shift went to two and three and many went on continuous seven-day operation much of the time.

This transition from peace-time operation to war production in a very real sense marked the end of executive leisure. Administrators were not affected by the President's executive order in the sense that they were required to punch the time clock for a longer day and week but they were affected much more, by high priority rush orders on the one hand and by scarce labor and materials on the other. The working day became a kind of struggle just to keep one's head above water.

The end of the war brought with it a hope—at least it did to me—that this feverish kind of activity would cease, that we could return to the more satisfactory and more leisurely pace of the thirties. From all that I can see, and hear, and experience, this has not happened; the demands made upon executives of every kind seem to be just as fierce today as they were during World War II.

To say this is to say nothing new, of course. On every hand we hear and talk about the swift tempo of modern living; we speak facetiously of the "ulcer factor"; we read

Horatio Alger-like articles about the 14-hour day put in by the president of General Motors; friends who hold executive positions say they are "in a rat race" or "on a merry-go-round"; physicians, themselves victims of the same mad rush, warn us to slow down, lest we have a coronary, a nervous breakdown, high blood pressure, arteriosclerosis, or an ulcer. Like the weather, everybody talks about it but no one does anything about it.

Various explanations of the phenomenon are offered: the high level of the economy, growth in the population, the power and recalcitrance of labor, the need to communicate, the scarcity of executive talent, migration to the suburbs, the disappearance of domestic servants, radio, television, the automobile, all are damned as responsible and all, no doubt, have something to do with the case. I propose to offer my own explanation, in hope that it will have at least a *soupçon* of therapeutic value.

2

A few years ago, at a lecture on operations research, I was introduced to something called "queueing theory," which proved to be the mathematical treatment of phenomena related to waiting lines of all sorts: automobiles at a toll gate, customers at a counter, phone calls at a switchboard, jobs at a machine, patients in a doctor's waiting room, etc., etc. During the course of his lecture, the speaker introduced the concept of an *arrival rate* and a *service rate*, these respectively being the rate at which cars, customers, phone calls, jobs, or patients arrive at the facility and the rate at which they are discharged or serviced.[1]

He then asked what would happen if arrivals were ran-

[1] Byron O. Marshall, "Queueing Theory," *Operations Research for Management*, Vol. I, pp. 134–148. Baltimore, The Johns Hopkins Press, 1954.

dom and if the arrival rate and service rate were exactly equal. My immediate inclination was to think that this would be ideal, the service facility would be kept continuously busy at minimum cost per unit of service rendered and nothing would have to wait. I was quite shocked when the speaker declared that under such conditions long queues would form and ultimately become infinite in length. His explanation was reasonably simple: because he had postulated a condition of random arrival, there would be some intervals during which there would be no arrivals and nothing to serve. During such times, the service facility would stand idle, its service capability for that period would be lost forever, and henceforth the service rate would be less than, rather than equal to, the arrival rate, and the queue would grow infinitely long.

This situation is depicted graphically in Fig. 10, where the ordinate represents the number of items waiting in queue and the abscissa the ratio of the arrival rate to the service rate. When these are equal the ratio $A/S = 1$ and the waiting line ultimately goes to infinity.

For a long time I was inclined to think of this as an intriguing but not very useful idea. Having had experience in scheduling jobs in industry, I knew that arrivals are not random but controlled; this is what we did when we took a new job and scheduled it through the plant, we controlled it, or, as I shall show, we thought we did. I also knew, as everyone does, that service rates do not remain fixed during times of peak load. They rise. Everyone works harder when there is more work to do: the toll gate attendant collects money and makes change at a quickened pace, the sales girl and the telephone operator become more expeditious, the worker sets-up and runs his machine a little faster, and the doctor becomes less inclined to in-

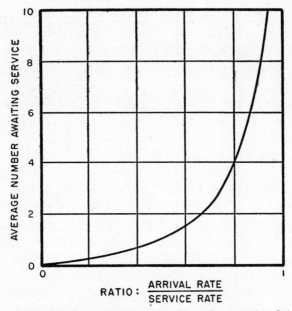

FIG. 10. Relationship between queue length with random arrivals and the ratio of arrival rate to service rate.

dulge in idle chit-chat with his patients. If we can control arrivals and if service rates can rise when necessary, the notion of infinite queues is of academic interest and not much more.

So I thought, until I listened to another lecture on the same subject, given by a colleague and friend, Charles Flagle.[2] On this occasion, by mathematical analysis, it was shown that when a controlled process decays, that is to say, when control of arrivals diminishes, the process itself tends to behave as though arrivals were random.

[2] Charles D. Flagle, "Models for Queueing Theory," *Proceedings of the Symposium on Operational Models*, Chemical Corps Engineering Command and Department of Mathematics, New York University. Published by Army Chemical Center, Maryland, 1957.

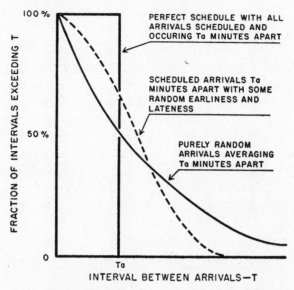

FIG. 11. Graphic portrayal of the decay of a controlled process.

The intervals between arrivals, no longer uniform, begin to resemble those in the purely random process. There are a great many short intervals, causing congestion, and a significant number of large ones, causing idleness at some times and at other times an opportunity to work off the backlog. This is depicted graphically in Fig. 11. This thesis, it may be remarked parenthetically, certainly fits experience. One has only to make an airline flight in bad weather to observe the somewhat chaotic "stacking" that takes place over airports when regular schedules are disrupted.

Learning this causes me to reflect about myself as a reasonably typical overloaded administrator and about my experience in industrial scheduling. Let me speak of the last first.

3

To illustrate what has been called the deification of numbers, a previous anecdote described the boss who wishfully converted a thousand unsold keyboard hours into an exact number, useful for managerial decision (page 84). As an outcome of that incident, I was given the task of devising a way to measure plant capacity and demand in order to gain the control which then was lacking.

The outcome of this effort need not be described in detail here; it will suffice to say that the new method did provide a means of measuring plant capacity as a rate with respect to time; it did provide a way to measure demand upon that capacity, also as a rate with respect to time; it showed the relative priority of each of the jobs in hand or in prospect; it provided for the subtraction of work done from demand; and it had means for adjustment up or down as capacity changed with growth or shrinkage.

In short, it established what was believed to be a controlled process. If a prospective new customer asked when his work could be completed, the salesman could not give him a guesswork reply but was compelled to abide by the schedule of available open time. If, as was more usual, the customer stated his own delivery needs, he could be told yea or nay only after the schedule had revealed whether or not the work could be done, or if shifts in priority could be made to accomplish what the customer wanted. It was *verboten* for anyone, even the president of the company, to make a delivery commitment contrary to the dictates of the schedule.

Despite this very firm policy, the schedule has never gained real control in the 15 years of its operation. Throughout this time the company has operated in a very strong seller's market, demand outruns capacity, the plant is almost continuously oversold, much work is done behind schedule, customers often are dissatisfied—and executives and the organization itself are overloaded.

As one of the originators of the method, I was, of course, strongly identified with its success or failure. In a certain sense, the schedule has succeeded: it has been in continuous use for about 15 years, management relies upon it and makes decisions in accordance with the measures it supplies. But in another, larger sense, the method has failed: it has not prevented either overload or delinquent work and it certainly has not relieved executives of the strain that goes with these conditions.

For a long time I did not know why and had a lurking sense of dissatisfaction about my own accomplishment. The measurement techniques appeared to be sound, the means for adding, deleting, or rescheduling jobs satisfactory, the presentation of data accurate, yet the schedule never gained control. Still puzzled after hearing the two lectures on queueing theory, I asked leave to describe the scheduling system before the same seminar, in the hope that someone in the audience could put his finger upon some basic flaw in the method.

Another of my colleagues, Eliezer Naddor, supplied the answer. "Do you," he said, "always endeavor to schedule up to capacity?" When I said yes, that unsold capacity is intolerable as long as there are sales to be made, he replied by saying, "Then you will always have an infinite queue." He meant this fancifully, of course, and not in the sense that a mathematician would use "infinite" but he did put his finger upon the cause of overload, the reason why the schedule could not achieve what it was intended to.

Consider again the second of the two queueing theory

postulates as it applies to this situation: *When a controlled process becomes less controlled, it tends to approach the behavior of a random process.* The schedule purported to establish control but really did not: manuscripts would not be received when due but often were late; proofs would be sent out and returned at times quite different from those specified and often they would contain many unanticipated author's alterations; precise schedules were as often upset as they were maintained. In short, the process exhibited a strong tendency away from control and therefore approached a random process in its behavior.

Couple with this the first queueing theory postulate: *When service rate and arrival rate are equal and when arrivals are random, a queue of infinite length will tend to form.* In the scheduling situation, arrival rate and service rate are made equal deliberately; unsold time being intolerable, the plant *always* is scheduled to 100 per cent of capacity. Arrival rate and service rate, one might say, are equal by definition. Under such circumstances, given a strong seller's market, scheduling to capacity, and some lack of control, the scheduling method is bound to fail, it cannot do otherwise, there *must* be an overload.

4

Very pretty, you may say, but still not very meaningful. One can always increase capacity by growing, indeed this is the desideratum, the *sine qua non* of American industry. Organizations must grow or retrogress, there is no such thing as standing still, so the platitude goes.

Very well, one *can* grow but this is no solution, unless growth is sufficient to absorb *all* of the demand and thereby convert a seller's market into a buyer's market. Until that happens, as long as there are jobs to sell and a policy of scheduling to capacity, the plant inexorably will be oversold, and the organization and its executives will be overloaded. When that happens, when a buyer's market compels scheduling below capacity, only then will the overload disappear. The company in question has expanded its operations again and again during the last decade; if anything, the overload today is worse than ever.

If increasing the service rate by expanding capacity will not work, we are left with no other choice but that of diminishing the arrival rate, granted that we want to get rid of overload. We must, in other words, schedule less work than we can do, keep some capacity in reserve, unsold. But this, in American business, is an intolerable, downright antisocial idea. One must never turn down an order or refuse a customer, the organization must always grow, this year must be bigger than last, so goes the creed of American business. To these aphorisms add the understandable distaste of labor for prospective short hours or layoff and the relationship between high volume, low costs, low prices, and good profits, and one can see that the industrial administrator is indeed on the horns of a dilemma. He may want with all his heart to escape organization overload and the stresses and strains that it imposes upon his people but the alternative choices available are not pretty ones. He can act, as he almost always does, to increase capacity but this will not solve the problem unless capacity can be made to exceed demand. Or, as he almost never does, he can diminish the arrival rate by deferring or turning down some of the work offered to him. This may solve the overload problem but will go against his own creed and probably play hob with his conscience.

5

So far, I have dealt chiefly with organization overload and have spoken of overload upon executives only as concomitant to their organization roles. Let me now use myself as an individual example of an overloaded professional person.

Like the company with the scheduling problem, I too operate in a kind of seller's market. I too think that I can control the arrival rate of commitments and determine their relative priorities but this is only partly true. I can control my schedule of classes and appointments of various kinds, and my secretary can use a desk calendar to predict commitments and, seemingly, to prevent overload. But there are always high priority, unanticipated demands which cause my personal "process" to "decay" and thereby approach a random process in nature and behavior. I am in the same boat as the company and must choose between the same ugly alternatives.

How do I respond to this overload? In just the same way as countless other administrators and professional people do, by working harder. An individual cannot increase capacity like a factory, by building a new plant or buying a faster machine, he can increase his service rate only by working faster or longer himself, and this is what he does.

Does this resolve the overload? No, no more than it did in the factory. If the demand for one's services is still there, increasing the service rate and then scheduling up to it, as one is inclined to do, will leave the overload untouched. Start to carry a brief case home to catch up in the evening and it will become routine. Commence working on weekends and this will soon become a habit. The new, expanded personal service rate will become the base—and the overload will still be there. If this sounds like the voice of experience, it is.

There is only one solution and that involves exactly the same struggle with creed and conscience that besets the business man who declines an order when his plant is not sold out. Let me receive an invitation to give a lecture somewhere and the inward struggle is on. If I have another, prior commitment I can refuse blithely. enough, with easy conscience, but, if my calendar is clear for the appointed time, I am loath to say no, even though I suspect that I shall be worn and harassed when the time comes to deliver. Perhaps I am beguiled by the flattery of being asked; by the prospect of being complimented as all speakers, even very poor ones, always are; by the honorarium which may be involved. Whatever the cause, it is a fact that to say no to such a request, without a good excuse, is to feel guilty of shirking one's duty. And to plead overwork or lack of time is simply not considered a good excuse, either to one's respondents or, more significantly, to one's self.

6

Throughout these pages, the argument has been as closely reasoned as I can make it but I do not wish to leave the impression that executive strain is a consequence solely of overload à la queueing theory. Decision making itself, which in a sense *is* administration, certainly has an "ulcer factor" and so does the rapid rate of change that characterizes modern industry and present day society. Apropos of this, a friend of mine in operations research once remarked that it took one man perhaps an hour, a day, or maybe a week to invent the long bow, and then this simple device became the dominant military weapon for many years. Nowadays, he went on to say, it takes hundreds of men ten years to develop a new airplane, which then be-comes obsolete on the day it is first flown. *Plus ça change, plus c'est la même chose* hardly applies to today's world.

Things of this kind and more besides no doubt contribute to executive overload. We cannot hope to obliterate them all and achieve a paradise of administrative tranquility. But I do believe that the precepts of queueing theory ex-plain one important cause of executive and organization overload and indicate the futility of doing more, just be-cause there is more to do. There is only one solution and that is to battle creed and conscience by learning to say no. Q.E.D.

XVII

On Organizations and Individuals

A YEAR or so ago, on a shopping trip to the local A. & P. store with my wife, I was detailed to get a half-dozen lemons, while she was making purchases at the meat counter. It was easy enough to pick up three lemons in each hand but then I wasn't sure whether they could be put into the cart loose or whether they were supposed to be bagged and priced by the boy at the green grocery counter, like the vegetables there usually were.

When I asked him he said no, and then just to make friendly conversation, I asked him if the Brothers Hartford would approve of loose lemons in a shopper's cart. "Who are they?" he said, very obviously not comprehending my question. When I told him that the Hartfords were the principal owners of the Great Atlantic and Pacific Tea Company, his response was amusing: "Oh," he said, "I always thought the A. & P. belonged to a Company."

This *is* amusing, to be sure, but it is also poignant, illustrating, as it does, how impersonal a vast organization can become. In the persons of his immediate superiors, this boy was working for other people but, beyond them, somewhere in the rarefied atmosphere at the top of the organization, there was only a "Company." Had I questioned him closely and had he stopped to think about it, I suppose he would have realized that there had to be people at the top too but his spontaneous comprehension certainly did not go that far. To him the A. & P. belonged to a Company.

Thus, organizations, particularly large ones, become re-mote and impersonal to those in or near the rank and file. The boy in the A. & P. bagged and priced vegetables and fruit, restocked his counters with new produce, and no doubt knew that money was collected for what was sold and paid for what was bought. He knew his boss, and the other boys, and the butchers and check-out girls too, and they were flesh and blood, understandable people, but beyond them and the environs of the store itself there was only some vast, incomprehensible system, which supplied the goods, took away the money, provided paychecks—and belonged to a Company.

All of us in various ways and degrees are in just the same situation as the A. & P. boy. We turn on and off the lights, use the telephone, find the milk and the newspaper on our doorsteps in the morning, set out the trash and, indeed, fulfill our jobs in organizations of various kinds without either understanding the complexities of the services we use or of the organizations we serve.[1]

The people with whom we have contact are real enough: the electric company repairman, the telephone operator, the milkman, our fellow employees, but the organizations behind them are likely to be remote and impersonal.

At the same time, perhaps because of this very absence of feeling or realization that the organization consists throughout of people, we endow the impersonal with personality. When we speak of "company policy" we are not consciously thinking of some regulation or procedure conceived and stated by an individual as a person, or by a group as a collection of persons. We are thinking more of a kind of dogma which emanated from the personified

[1] Gordon W. Allport has commented upon this in "The Psychology of Participation," *Human Factors in Management*. Parkville, Mo., Park College Press, 1946.

organization itself—from "the Company." The case previously recounted about the employee deprived of holiday pay (p. 54) is an instance of this very thing.

Similarly, to the enlisted man and to a great many officers, "Army Regulations" do not mean a set of rules made by men and capable of being changed by men; they are a set of rules made by the Army itself. "University standards," "Union Laws," "Government Regulations," all have this same characteristic: that they are made by men tends to be forgotten; they are ascribed to the personified organizations themselves.

2

My purpose in saying this is not to emphasize again the inflexible, dogmatic nature of rules, for this was done in Chapter VI (p. 52). Nor do I hope to change or diminish the personification of organizations, for such a hope would be ill founded. Terms like "the Company," "the Bank," "the Navy," "the Police Department" are much too deeply rooted and much too convenient in use ever to be eradicated. My purpose is only to argue that the wisest administrative policy is that which consistently is best for each of the individuals who comprise the organization.

This requires a word of explanation and qualification. One could say, for instance, that the *best* thing the A. & P. could do for the grocery boy would be to give him all the receipts and thereby make him rich and independent. But this, of course, would bankrupt and destroy the organization and would be very bad for all of the other individuals, toward whom the policy also is directed. One must say therefore that the wisest administrative policy is that which consistently is best for each of the individuals who comprise the organization and, at the same time, consonant with the needs and objectives of the organization itself, that is to say, of *all* of the individuals who comprise the organization. This considers organization as an aggregation of *people*, not merely as a *thing*.

In espousing such a policy, I am not so sanguine as to believe that regard for the individual will at once transform "the Company" into something warm and personal from top to bottom. General Motors would still be General Motors, gigantic and incomprehensible to the man on the assembly line, even if his wants and needs were given the very maximum of consideration. The grocery boy in the A. & P. would still think that the vast chain of stores belonged to a "Company," even though policy were directed toward that which was best for *him*.

But there would be a difference. Let an incident arise which involves a conflict or seeming conflict between some individual and the organization itself. Let decision be made by an executive who worships the god of organization. The result will enhance the *im*personality of the organization.

Contrariwise, let the same incident arise but now have the executive ask himself: "What can I do in this matter which is best for the employee and also compatible with the interest of the organization?" The decision with this approach may not always be different but sometimes it will and, when it is, the personality of the organization, the fact that it is composed of people after all, will to some degree be emphasized.

And, as I propose also to argue by way of examples, the decision made will be better, not only for the individual but for the organization itself.

3

In the academic world, promotion of a member of the faculty is supposed to depend upon a variety of factors: teaching competence, research achievement, publications, reputation in the field of specialization, age and seniority, the judgment of colleagues, etc. In some institutions of higher learning, where research is greatly esteemed, achievement in research, evaluated by the number and quality of publications, tends to become the dominant criterion for promotion and, indeed, for retention on the faculty at a given subordinate rank. Expressed with a shade of difference, the promotion of an assistant professor or associate professor to the next higher rank is more easily accomplished for a candidate of doubtful teaching competence but who has an impressive research and publication record, than it is for a superb teacher who has no bibliography by which to show his research attainments. This is not perhaps the way things ought to be, as I have already said in discussing the deification of numbers (p. 97), but it is the way things are.

Not so very long ago, under circumstances of this kind, the promotion of a young assistant professor was proposed by his immediate superior, the department chairman, and a committee was formed in the usual way to gather pertinent information and recommend yea or nay to the governing board.

A review of the candidate's qualifications, some of which were already known to members of the committee, revealed that his academic history had been one of unmixed success; through high school, college and graduate school he had not only been outstanding as a student but also as a leader. Both his scholarly and leadership capabilities were accompanied by wisdom as well as knowledge, a most agreeable personality, good character, and a fine appearance.

His stature as a lecturer and teacher was equally good. This was known from comments made by students from time to time and also by some members of the faculty who had heard him lecture on various occasions. I have heard him myself and can testify to his ability to make complex subjects clear by extraordinarily lucid and straightforward presentation.

But the committee also found, to their considerable surprise, that he had written and published precisely nothing in the years during which he had held appointment as assistant professor. In the face of this, and the kind of evaluation previously described, promotion to associate professor was deemed impossible. Again it may be argued that the evaluation criteria are wrong, that a teacher of such outstanding capability deserved promotion, with or without publications. Again, I can agree most heartily but that does not alter the fact: without research and consequent publications this most worthy candidate could not be promoted.

In the face of such a reality, it would have been easy for the committee simply to bring in a report recommending against promotion. Since promotions are never made by the governing board without a favorable recommendation, it would have been easy for that body to deny the request made by the candidate's department chairman. Then, if the chairman had been a devout worshiper of the god of organization, it would have been easy for him to say to his subordinate, "Sorry, no publications, no promotion."

Happily, none of these routine things occurred. Knowing

the potential capabilities of the candidate, the chairman of the committee first set about trying to discover why the young man had published nothing about the research he had done. He finally learned that his doctoral dissertation had been submitted for publication a few years back and had been severely—and rather unjustifiably—criticized by the editorial referee to whom it had been submitted. This rebuff, falling as it did upon a cherished dissertation, had created a kind of mental block, a resistance to writing for publication and attendant exposure to possible criticism.

In the discussions which followed this disclosure, four people, two in administration and two on the faculty, separately and independently voiced the same question: "What can be done that is best for this man?" It was decided that the committee chairman, a senior member of the faculty of stature and wisdom, would seek by a series of conferences to remove the mental block and encourage and assist in the preparation of the necessary papers. It is yet too soon to report the results which are hoped for.

Those who read this anecdote can say, with some justification, that it is trivial. The promotion standards themselves are phony and the argument that the action was best for the organization itself is obvious: in these days of growing college population, teachers are scarce and staff is hard to get, therefore the executives concerned were only seeking to protect themselves and were not really concerned with what was best for the individual.

This may be good rationalization but it does not agree with the context. The action taken in this particular case was characteristic of so many others that it is safe to say that a policy of attention to the individual is a constant goal in this institution. When a student fails, especially at a time when there are so many students, it is easy to say,

"Off with his head!" and drop him from college. This is quick and easy, susceptible to rule making and quantification (three failures and you're out), and virtuous, because it keeps precious academic standards high. It is much more time consuming, much more difficult, much more demanding—but much better—to ask why he has failed and what can be done to bring about his salvation. The number who are "saved" by this conscious emphasis upon the individual is surprising, and also gratifying.

4

A case of the opposite kind can also be recounted.

During World War II, a young man, but recently married to a fellow employee in an industrial concern, was drafted into the Seabees and sent to a post in the South for basic training. A few weeks later he was able to send for his wife; she requested her vacation, received approval for it, and left to join her husband.

Once there, near her husband's base, she learned that he would be there for several months before being sent to the South Pacific, and that she could get a civilian job as secretary-typist in a nearby Army camp. She applied, was accepted, and the Army officer concerned telegraphed to her former employers for a "release."

In those days of labor scarcity, to prevent employers from pirating workers successively from one another and to prevent employees from "job hopping" to the greener pastures of higher wages, more overtime, or more glamorous jobs, there was a War Labor Board order which forbade an employer to hire a worker from another organization without the aforesaid release. The order also said that employers should not give releases willy-nilly but should follow a general principle: if the worker already was employed at his or her "highest skill" in an "essential industry," the release should be denied. An employee could quit his or her job at any time he or she desired but, without a release, could not get another job in an essential industry until 60 days had passed.

Obviously, a good deal of latitude had to be exercised in seeking to obey this regulation or we would have had something approaching involuntary servitude. Releases sometimes were given to employees simply because they were so recalcitrant or so unhappy in their jobs as to make them almost worthless as workers. Releases sometimes were withheld from employees who appeared to want another job just to evade the draft.

In this particular case, the telegram requesting a release for the wife thoroughly enraged the executive in charge. This was understandable enough; he was beset by the compounded troubles of high production demand and scarce labor supply, he had given the girl her vacation to be with her husband, and now she was trying to escape, thus depriving him of a skilled machine operator he could not replace. The needs of the organization completely transcended the needs of the individual in his telegraphed reply: "Mrs. X employed at her highest skill in essential industry. Release denied."

A few days later he received a letter from the husband, which was throughout a passionate denunciation of the company in general and the executive in particular. The young Seabee husband pointed out that he would soon be sent overseas, possibly into combat, certainly into hazard, and that he and his bride intended to be together as many of the hours left to them as possible. He called the executive a dictator and a Little Hitler and said that it was against just such people as he that the war was being fought. Mrs. X, of course, stayed with her husband and, presumably, was hired by the Army without a release.

In this case it is very easy to argue that consideration of the individual would have resulted in a decision better for the organization, as well as for the two employees. As it was, the company lost Mrs. X's services anyway, incurred the wrath of both of them and, no doubt, lost esteem in the eyes of other workers too, since the story got about among them.

There was, happily, a pleasant sequel. The executive was and is to some extent over-devoted to the organization and tends to expect comparable devotion from his associates. (I once crossed swords with him by saying that the organization existed for *me*, not I for it.) He has always worked extremely hard and during the war gave of himself unstintingly, in a sincere and genuinely patriotic way. It was only natural, therefore, for him to react as he did to the request for release.

But beneath the surface of this over-devotion to the organization there was also compassion and understanding. The letter from X hit home and hurt badly and could have brought retaliation. He showed me the letter—a very courageous act in itself—and I know the hurt it gave. I do not know the reply the executive sent but can gauge its nature from the result: both Mr. and Mrs. X returned to work at the plant after the war. As far as I know, X is still there.

5

These two cases, in a way, represent extremes: in the university, the needs of the individual came first; in the plant, the needs of the organization were dominant. In the first case, the economy of a policy of doing what is best for the individual is difficult to show; in the second, the economy of giving a release willingly is evident. Between these kinds of extremes, and occurring much more frequently, is a whole class of cases involving more difficult administrative decisions.

In 1929, for example, the Texas and Pacific Railroad abandoned Longview Junction and Marshall as freight terminals and established a new freight terminal at Mineola, Texas. "Longview was a town of about 6,000 or 7,000. It was estimated that the transfer of the train and engine service employees and their families from Longview to Mineola would produce an immediate loss of approximately 1,000 in the population of Longview. The result would be a serious depreciation in the value of the property owned and occupied by the employees affected. The employees demanded compensation for these losses. After a refusal of the employees to accept the railroad company's offer to arbitrate, President Hoover, on March 29, 1929, created an Emergency Board, under sec. 10 of the Railway Labor Act. The Emergency Board held: 'The change from Longview Junction to Mineola and from Marshall to Shreveport will result in a substantial saving for the carrier. It is not fair, we think, that the carrier reap the entire benefit and that the employees be compelled to bear the entire loss.' The Board held that the loss should be borne equally by the carrier and the employees. The loss, according to the Board, would be the difference in the market value of the property just before it became generally known that the terminal would be moved, and the market value immediately after removal." (*Report of the Emergency Board, Transmitting its Findings upon the Dispute between*

Texas and Pacific Railway Company and Certain Engine and Train Service Employees.)[2]

One can say quite easily in retrospect that it would have been more economical for the railroad to have paid voluntarily rather than by Emergency Board order but an important administrative question remains unanswered: how far should an organization go in doing what is best for the individuals who comprise it? This same question arises frequently, as the following narratives will show.

A manufacturing organization in the New England area employed a watchman who was a Navy veteran of both World Wars. His ship had been torpedoed in World War I but he had then escaped injury. In World War II he met with the same fate but this time he was less fortunate: he lost a leg. With this infirmity, he could not perform his old job and the company, in effect, created one for him, making him watchman on the night turn.

Possibly because of his combat experience, possibly because of an unhappy home environment, the man became an alcoholic. His drinking presented recurrent problems to his superior, of absence, lateness, and incapacity, climaxed by his hitting the boss with his cane when he was sent home too drunk to work. For this he was fired. His union asked reinstatement but this was denied by me in the capacity of arbitrator.

Prior to this dramatic climax, the company had made considerable effort on behalf of the individual, consciously placing his welfare first. He had received extensive and extended medical care, his family had been visited, other jobs had been tried, and he had patiently been forgiven a whole series of transgressions. With the caning of his boss, management at last decided that his needs no longer were

[2] Sumner S. Slichter, *Union Policies and Industrial Management*, p. 133, footnote. Washington, D.C., The Brookings Institution, 1941.

consonant with those of the organization and he was discharged. Thus, in effect, he was changed from being a ward of the company to being a ward of his family, or of society as a whole.

Similarly, in another mid-western branch of this same company, an employee fell downstairs at home and broke his arm. Osteomyelitis developed and the fracture refused to heal. Over a period of nearly two years this man, whose injury was not job-incurred and therefore not compensable under the Workmen's Compensation Act, received full salary for thirteen weeks and medical and hospital care costing, in all, about $4,000, an amount only slightly less than his aggregate earnings throughout his entire period of employment by the company. At a time when he was about to have yet another operation paid for by the company insurance plan, the company decided that his extended sick leave and insurance coverage would be terminated after the operation then in prospect.

Again the union brought the grievance to arbitration, asking that the injured man be retained on the sick list, and again the arbitrator ruled in favor of the company.

These cases of incapacities through alcoholism and injury, and the Texas and Pacific case as well, are illustrative of a whole class of administrative decisions which concern individuals: How far should a business or industrial organization go on behalf of an individual who is derelict in some way in the performance of his job? How far should an academic organization go in giving "one more chance" to delinquent students who are believed to have intellectual competence but who fail to perform because of inadequate motivation, emotional conflict, or any of the many distractions affecting young people? How far should the armed forces go in doing what is best for the individual who resists the regimentation characteristic of military organizations? Each of these questions asks what the organization should do but in every such case it is the administrators who must decide.

There is no categorical, unequivocal answer, of course. My own opinion is that the administrator should go pretty far, having his policy centered, as I have said before, upon what is best for the individual and consonant with the organization needs, rather than vice versa. But when it becomes apparent that the incapacity or dereliction of the industrial worker cannot be changed, when the delinquent student stays delinquent, when the resistant soldier stays resistant, decisions must be made against them or the organization itself will be endangered. In the last analysis, organizations like these are not and should not be therapeutic institutions.

6

There is another way of looking at these problems in economic terms. Retention of the alcoholic on the payroll, plus provision of medical and sociological services for him, costs money, which would be saved by discharging him upon his first offense. The purpose of the organization is the manufacture of product, not the cure of alcoholism, therefore prompt discharge is the only right decision.

But the organization also has several hundred other employees, many of whom know the night watchman and his war record. Their sentiments, their good will or ill will toward the company, have value. If they are favorably disposed toward the organization, they may work a bit harder, put out a bit more, attend more regularly and punctually, be more inclined to keep their jobs. If, conversely, they do not like the company, they may complain and criticize both on and off the job, work a little less, and leave a little sooner.

We cannot measure the aggregate of these sentimental values but logically we must at least admit the possibility that their sum can exceed the more easily measured costs of medical services. If, by discharging the watchman on his first offense, we incur the ill will of other employees; if the sum of this ill will leads to costs greater than the cost of medical care, then discharge is a poor decision—and is poor on strictly economic grounds.

Evaluation is yet more subtle than this. The sentimental values are not only immeasurable, they are altered up or down but are not wholly created by single incidents nor by single decisions. Suppose, for example, that the watchman is fired forthwith on first offence, but grant that the aggregate cost of ill will generated by the act is less than the costs of retention. Is the discharge decision then economically sound?

Not necessarily. The negative sentiments to which value has been ascribed will become a part of the total image of the company held by the employees. That image of the company as a good or bad place to work will be negatively affected by decisions which seemingly are inhumane and positively affected by those which seemingly are humane. Thus, when the next decision to discharge or to discipline is made, its economic evaluation will have a different base, one that is less advantageous to the company.

The converse of this is also true, of course. Let the watchman be retained and good will is enhanced, at the cost of providing medical care. Let him transgress again and be retained again, and let this be repeated several times. Each time the company's forbearance, patience, and tolerance will add to the cost of retention but enhance total good will. Then, when the decision to discharge is made and, what is more, made with provocation, any loss of good will is likely to be negligible. Indeed, perhaps paradoxically, the good will of the other employees may be increased at such a time.

These arguments have been fanciful in more ways than one. Accountants might scoff at the notion of incurring medical and sociological costs by retaining the watchman, on the ground that these are fixed elements of cost which are provided by the company anyway. This is true enough in the short run but the fact does not alter the case; it merely strengthens the argument.

It may also seem fanciful to speak, even paradoxically, of enhancing employee good will by the act of discharge, when union intervention for reinstatement has been reported, an act which certainly bespeaks employee *ill* will, if anything. Again, not necessarily. Unions are essentially political organizations and often they must interfere at the time of *any* discharge, just to show their constituents that they are alert on their behalf. The reader must accept my report that there was not much militance nor too much vigor on behalf of the discharged watchman.

Regardless of the fancy in these arguments, they do have substance. They urge doing what is best for the individual on the ground that this can be best for the organization as well. This is a humane policy but it is also an economic one, because acting on behalf of the individual incurs costs and affects values. When, in the judgement of the administrator, the sum of the costs is deemed to exceed the sum of the values, action *against* the individual is in order.

All of these many pages, in effect, say only one thing: to the administrator and to the organization or segment of organization he directs, the Golden Rule has more than human value. It has economic value as well.

XVIII

On Criteria for Decisions

IN THE game of lacrosse, which is very popular hereabouts, it was customary a long time ago for defense players to cut off the handles of their sticks at lengths which would just come to the level of the armpit, when the stick was stood upon the ground. Nowadays this custom has changed, now defense players use much longer sticks, so much longer that the committee on rules has seen fit to ordain a maximum permissible length of six feet. Some sticks appear to exceed even this.

During the course of a game a year or two ago, from the awkward performance of some of the players, it seemed to me that six feet might not be an optimum length at all; what defense men gain in defending facility and reach by using long sticks might be more than counterbalanced by what they lose in lightness and maneuverability. It occurred to me that this question might make an interesting study in human engineering and I proposed it to a student, who did indeed become intrigued by the idea.

His proposed experimental design to test this hypothesis was intended to simulate various aspects of the game and to measure the performance of a number of player-subjects. Thus, capability for recovering loose balls from the ground could be measured with both long and short sticks by repeating the simulation sufficiently often to get statistically valid measures of successes and failures. Similarly, throwing from standing and running positions could be measured, so could catching, speed of movement, etc. Simulation of defending capabilities would have been more difficult but, still, it could have been done.

When the idea was broached to the coaching staff, they were responsive enough but their general attitudes reflected a point of view which is quite germane to the administrative process. Suppose that you can measure these separate attributes, they argued in effect, how can you possibly weigh them in such a way as to get a definite answer? Suppose that a short stick does prove to be measurably better for catching and throwing but poorer for defending, how shall you relate these conflicting qualities in order to reach a decision? Expressed with more sophistication, how can the results be synthesized into a perfect decision?

The answer, of course, is that the results cannot be synthesized into a perfect decision. But to this answer there are two relevant responses:

1. Defense players *already* have made their decisions by the adoption and use of long sticks. They have done this from intuition, from experience, but most of all from following the examples of others. They have made no measurements but they have nonetheless made firm decisions.

2. The question, therefore, is not whether simulation experiments can yield a *perfect* answer or a *perfect* synthesis but only whether they can yield a *better* one. An important criterion, then, applicable to all decision making, is not perfection but only relative goodness.

Trivial and perhaps nonsensical as this example is, the rationale involved is no different from that needed in countless decision making situations. Time study, as pointed out before (p. 88), yields less than perfect measurements of operation performance. For this lack of perfection, time study has been attacked and criticized from every side but the fact remains that no industrial administrator can estimate a cost, or give a schedule, or evaluate the performance of his workers—in short, he cannot operate his enterprise—without predictions of operation time requirements. Time study is not a perfect means of measurement but that is *not* the question. Time study should be carried out as well as can be and, when it is, is a better—in fact, the best presently available—means of taking measurements that must be taken for decisions that must be made. That *is* the question.

The same argument applies to the computer tank battles also described in an earlier chapter (pp. 91–94). The results of such computer simulations can be perfectly synthesized no more than measurements of long and short lacrosse sticks. But to equip an army, decisions must be made about what kinds of tanks to buy. These are momentous decisions but they are basically no different from the trivial one of deciding how long a stick to use in order to play a game of lacrosse. If the computer can yield a better answer than other ways of deciding upon military equipment, even if it can only assist in arriving at better decisions, it should be used.

Other measurement techniques used in the management of an organization are subject to the same considerations of relative goodness. Organization charts, job evaluation, accounting, merit rating, standard operating procedures, quality control, forecasting, planning, operations research, etc., all yield much less than perfect answers. I would not have their results deified, as I have already argued, nor would I have the costs of measuring ignored, but neither would I have these aids to decision making eschewed or abandoned on the ground of imperfection. Decisions made with them can be and usually are better than those made without them. *Better* is the key word.

2

In making decisions administrators are compelled to make choices between the relative worth of alternatives, and such alternatives *always* present conflicting values.

If profit is high in a business organization, shall it be distributed to stockholders as dividends, or shall it be kept in the enterprise? If it is decided to keep the dividend rate low, shall the funds be retained as working capital, or invested in replacement equipment, or spent to expand the plant?

What shall be done about wages and salaries? If they are kept at status quo, costs will be kept stable and competitive position maintained. But the labor force may become disaffected, may slow down, may unionize, may strike. To prevent this, let wages be raised. This will please the workers—provided the raise is sufficient—but now costs will go up and introduce yet another difficult decision: shall prices be raised? If this is done and sales remain high, profit may continue to be good. But *will* sales remain high?

Turn to any other kind of organization and find the same kinds of administrative choices. Should Meade have pursued the retreating Confederates after Gettysburg or have rested his weary soldiers? General Meade elected to remain where he was and thereby received the censure of history. Perhaps he made a bad decision—hindsight, it is said, is always 20-20—but it was at least an understandable one involving powerful conflicting values.

Farther down the military scale, how severe shall the drill sergeant be with his recruits? If he drives them too hard, their spirit may break; they may even rebel. If he tends to mollycoddle them, they will be too soft and may pay forfeit with their lives upon the field of battle.

Analogously, how fast shall the teacher go and how rigorous shall he be with his students? Let him go too fast or be too demanding and his students will learn nothing; let him go too slow and they will learn much less than they can or should. Even clergymen are subject to conflicting values of the same kind. Let them try to impose too strict a moral code upon their congregations and parishioners (i.e., their subordinates) and their missions will fail. This is an administrative decision and they too must walk a tightrope between too much and too little.

In integrated solutions to administrative problems there are these selfsame conflicting values. To reinstate Rollins in the recommended manner (p. 133), the executive would have had to weigh the potential gains against the possibility that theft might appear to be condoned. In the keyboard case described in Chapter II, integration could be achieved only by an initial admission that the standard set by the company might be wrong and an admission of managerial fallibility is not easy to make. The same conflicting values would have arisen in the ball bearing dispute (pp. 134–142) had integration been thought of there.

A too familiar aphorism says, apropos of business organizations, that administrators have the goal of maximizing profit. They do but not in the unlimited sense in which the aphorism is always stated. The business executive will seek to maximize profit over the long run but, as I have already indicated with respect to dividend decisions, investment decisions, wage decisions, and price decisions, he will be compelled to seek an optimum, rather than a maximum decision, for any given year. It is *now* when such decisions must be made.

In the same way a military commander seeks to maximize the chance of victory in war. But during the course of any given engagement or battle, he is concerned with decisions now. He will want to win that engagement or that battle but he will not be able to suppress the conflicting thought that "he who fights and runs away may live to fight another day."

There are no decisions which do not involve these conflicting values. Most of the time the sum of one set of values will greatly exceed the sum of those which are contrary and in all of these cases decisions will be easy. But often this is not the case, often the pro and con values are nearly balanced. When this is so, decisions are difficult. In either case the conflicting values are *always* present.

3

In a very large number of decisions, the alternative choices lie between incurring costs or risks now against the possibility of larger aggregate gains in the future. Let me illustrate by an example which comes very close to home.

What kind of decision shall I make if a letter comes to my desk describing an attractive position for which one of my own staff members is admirably suited? Shall I show the letter to my subordinate or give his name to the inquirer? Obviously, if I do give his name, I may either lose him to the competition and be compelled to seek a replacement, or I may have to seek a promotion for him in order to persuade him to stay. Both of these alternatives cost time and money but there is a potential return upon the investment: the staff man in question and his colleagues as well will know, if disclosure is made, that the organization is interested in them as individuals, which, as I have said before, has value. If the man in question does stay, with or without added emolument, his attachment and devotion to the organization will have a stronger bond.

Concealment of the opportunity has opposite costs and risks. If the man does not hear of the position, well and good, no cost has been incurred nor any gain made in organization morale. If the man hears of the chance by other means, he is more likely to be lost than if he hears of it from me. If he hears about the opportunity otherwise and then learns that it was known and concealed by his superior, the likelihood of his departure will be high and there will be damage to morale too.

In all of these considerations the only dollars involved are those which might be required to hold the man, if disclosure of the prospective position is made. Despite the fact that dollars are not dominant, the decision is essentially an economic one. A policy of disclosing such opportunities should not be favored just because the administrator wishes to be popular with his subordinates (although executive popularity does have value) but only if the sum of the values in a policy of disclosure is believed to exceed the sum of the values in a policy of concealment. The problem is essentially economic: whether to invest in disclosure for possible future gains in morale, or to withhold investment for possible present gain in successful concealment.[1]

[1] Since this was written the following comment has been received from Mr. P. Stewart Macaulay: ". . . I find the argument surrounding (this) example excessively hardboiled. In a situation such as this must the administrator act decently only if the 'sum of the values' . . . indicates that decency pays? Should not integrity or ethical considerations be elements in the case even though they may result in economic loss? Or, conversely cannot one place a high enough economic value on these virtues to force the scale to tip on the side of decency?"

With this comment I could not agree more fully. Indeed, it was my intent to argue that what might well be called the "economy of ethics" *is* overriding, *is* sufficient to tip the scale on the side of decency. I am greatly obliged for a comment which gives sharper point to the argument.

Industry affords an analogous example. Suppose that a jobbing manufacturer has produced but not yet delivered a quantity of sub-standard goods. Shall he approach the customer who gave him the order with a proposal for cut-price sale, or shall he voluntarily do the work over? There are shades and degrees of defects and shades and degrees of customer relations, so no categorical answer is possible. The conflicting values may be stated, however, in general terms.

If the manufacturer elects to do the work over, especially if this is a policy decision, he will incur the cost of re-work and loss on the order but he will receive a return upon his investment in the future: his customer will know and respect his policy and is likely to be bound closer as a customer; his own employees also will know that their company will not tolerate sub-standard product and this will motivate more careful work by them and a measure of added pride too. An administrator would not be wise to create spoilage just to show that this is his policy but he can sometimes make good use of the investment values inherent in such unfortunate occurrences.

Use of the word *investment* here and elsewhere has been deliberate. Usually, the word defines dollars spent for plant, equipment, or operations, or for securities, where there is expectation of future return upon money spent now. A larger but quite analogous meaning is intended here. The administrator *invests* in disclosing opportunities to his staff in the belief that this will yield future values which exceed the cost and risk of present disclosure. The manufacturer *invests* in doing spoiled work over for the same reason. My own opinion is that this capability to incur present cost and risk for future gains, especially when present cost and risk are real and apparent and future gains nebulous, is an essential characteristic of a good administrator. Certainly, every administrator confronts hundreds of issues of just this kind.

Parson Weems taught this same lesson in his story of George Washington and the cherry tree. Paradoxically, the Parson did not tell the truth himself about young George's investment in honesty but the lesson is a good one anyway.

4

"Politics," I once heard President Kirk of Columbia University say, "is the art of the possible." Except perhaps for those in public life, most administrators would not want to be known as politicians because of the distasteful connotations of the word. But in the sense of President Kirk's definition, every administrator must be a politician; he is perforce a decision maker and every decision is concerned with feasibility, with what is possible.

Again we come to a subtle distinction which helps to identify the good administrator: he will be sensitive to what he *can* do and will make feasible decisions which can be carried out, recognizing that to decide in favor of what he *cannot* do will impair his chance of doing anything at all—and will, besides, impair his reputation as a wise administrator.

To illustrate this, clinical examples are a little hard to come by. What is deemed quite feasible by one executive may be regarded as difficult by another, as very difficult by a third, and as impossible by a fourth. One must go to extremes to make the point.

Recently I read Sir Arthur Bryant's "The Turn of the Tide,"[1] a history based upon the diaries kept by Field-Marshal Lord Alanbrooke, Chief of the Imperial General Staff of the British Army during World War II. The book is high in its praise of both Alanbrooke and Churchill but, as I read, I became less and less impressed with Churchill's capabilities as an administrator, despite the near-adulation of the author for him.

Throughout the entire period of Alanbrooke's service as C.I.G.S. much of his energy was consumed in dissuading his superior from making rash decisions which literally were impossible to carry out. Again and again Churchill insisted upon a landing in Norway, an operation which would have required air cover, landing craft, naval forces, and troops, immense resources, none of which were then available. Even if such an expedition could get ashore successfully, there was, in Alanbrooke's view, no place to go.

As quickly as Churchill was talked out of this particular scheme, he would insist upon another: a landing in the Balkans, a premature offensive in North Africa, yet another landing in Norway. His demands for an attack, almost any attack it sometimes seemed, were relentless; they put very great strain upon the energies of his principal subordinate—and they were all impossible of execution. My opinion of Churchill as an administrator fell considerably as a consequence of reading a book in praise of him.

This is an anomaly and so, in a sense, is the example itself. Feasibility, as a criterion of decision making, has been introduced by a definition of politics. Sir Winston

[1] New York, Doubleday & Company, Inc., 1957.

Churchill is certainly one of the foremost politicians of the 20th Century, yet I have criticized him for the very thing in which, by definition, he might be deemed pre-eminent.

However, this need not be so. Churchill's very real greatness probably derives much more from the combination of great eloquence and great courage than from his skill as a decision maker. Throughout the entire war he was the very personification of his country, of the spirit of freedom, of opposition to tyranny, an asset of incalculable value to Great Britain and to ourselves. But as a decision maker, no, here he lacked perception of the art of the possible. For this opinion I am sure he could not care less.

A more down-to-earth example than this is in order. About 1946, when war-time measures to restrain inflation were removed, a local union in a large city presented an aggregation of demands which could only be described as fantastic. I am not sure that I remember details correctly but the following will serve to give the flavor of the union's proposals:

Wage rates for skilled craftsmen in the industry were then about $1.75 per hour; the union asked for $3.00.

Overtime was being paid at time and one-half for work in excess of 40 hours per week or eight per day; the union demanded that overtime be paid beyond 35 hours per week or seven per day and also that double time be paid for more than two hours overtime on any given day.

The existing contract called for holiday pay for all of our usual major holidays; the union asked for such pay on ten specified holidays. I cannot remember all of the days named but a few of them were the approximate equivalent of Samuel Gompers' Birthday, Flag Day, or the like. That is about the only way that ten holidays *can* be named.

For work done on any holiday, triple time pay was asked.

Three weeks' vacation with pay was demanded for relatively short-service employees, of five years' service as I recall it, and four weeks for ten years' service or more.

I have never been a party to the formulation of union demands for collective bargaining but strongly suspect that these would be deemed unwise even in organizations where inordinate demands seem to be the rule. Certainly, the chances of winning gains for employees would be diminished rather than enhanced by demands such as these. Furthermore, in the eyes of other union administrators, those who formulated these demands would be bound to lose status through their failure to appreciate the art of the possible. It is much better to ask for what there is at least a chance of getting.

5

So far in this chapter criteria for decisions have included the concept of relative goodness rather than perfection, the ever-presence of conflicting values, the "investment" character of many decisions, and the political quality of feasibility. Elsewhere the social and historical framework of administrative decisions has been discussed, along with compulsion to decide, the significance of null decisions, the sometimes futility of logic, and the irreversibility and irrevokability of many administrative actions.

These do not comprise all criteria for decision making nor am I capable of making such a compilation. Nor do these items suggest the dynamic nature of the administrative environment, where one decision can lead to another and another and another, in ceaseless, interlocking, and interdependent succession. Through these the administrator must thread his way, steering a course between Scylla on the one hand and Charybdis on the other, conscious that a crisis-making blunder may cost him his job and perhaps his executive reputation.

In our society administrators are accorded position, prestige, and handsome compensation. So also are those who paint, write, compose, act, sing, or play with skill. Some who can do these things exceptionally well are deservedly recognized as artists. That is what a good administrator is too—an artist.

Index